F | DATE DUE | |
---|---|---|---|
| | | |
| | | |
| | | |
| | | |
| | | |
| | | |
| | | |
| | | |
| | | |
| | | |

The Bible as Literature

a selective bibliography

A
Reference
Publication
in
Literature

Ronald Gottesman
Editor

The Bible as Literature

a selective bibliography

John H. Gottcent

G.K.HALL&CO.

70 LINCOLN STREET, BOSTON, MASS.

Library of Congress Cataloging in Publication Data

Gottcent, John H
    The Bible as literature.

    (A Reference publication in literature)
    Includes index.
    1. Bible as literature—Bibliography.   I.   Title.
II.   Series.
Z7770.G68   [BS535]   016.2206   79-17450
ISBN 0-8161-8121-7

This publication is printed on permanent/durable acid-free paper
MANUFACTURED IN THE UNITED STATES OF AMERICA

To Mom and Dad,
JoAnne, Caryn, Heidi,
and Stephen

sine qua non

Contents

Introduction

Recently, interest in the Bible as a literary work has developed among both biblical scholars and "secular" literary critics. Among the scholars, the trend has been shown by a renewed concern with biblical language and holistic approaches to narratives. Among the critics, it is seen both in the increasing number of courses in this subject at the secondary and collegiate levels (Indiana University, which has sponsored an annual Summer Institute on Teaching the Bible as Literature for almost ten years, now plans to implement a Ph.D. minor in the field), and in the slow but steady increase of publications in the area. However, a gap still separates the two groups: scholars are not exactly sure what literary critics do, and critics usually have little or no training in biblical studies.

This book attempts to bridge that gap. It is a selective annotated bibliography of materials useful to those interested in the Bible as literature who are looking for a place from which to begin an investigation of the field. Though it should be useful to both biblical scholars and literary critics, it is aimed primarily at those trained in secular literary studies--researchers, teachers at the collegiate and secondary levels, and students--since their training and research tools have more often tended to ignore this subject.

A Definition of the Field

It might be wise to define "the Bible as literature" before proceeding. Though different people working in the field will naturally place different emphases, the general definition on which this book is based sees the discipline as the treatment of the Bible or any of its parts in the way critics and teachers of literature treat secular literary works: by focusing on plot, characterization, structure, and uses of language--irony, metaphor, allusion, imagery, rhythm--as they contribute to theme. (For introductions to the more traditional scholarly approaches to the Bible, see section 3A.)

Though this definition somewhat overlaps the more traditional concerns of theologians and scholars, there are at least two major differences. First, theologians are primarily concerned with using the Bible to explain or defend points of dogma; literary critics, in contrast, tend to see themes from a more human perspective. Thus, in looking at the story of Abraham's sacrifice of Isaac in Genesis 22, the theologian, emphasizing hermeneutics, may focus on what the story reveals about faith and man's relationship to God in the modern world. The literary critic is more likely to concentrate on the psychological dimensions of Abraham's character, or the structure of the narrative, or what the language reveals about the human interactions and struggles; he may even see God as a "character" and analyze Him in much the same way as he does Abraham.

Second, the biblical scholar is primarily concerned with matters of history: he sees his job as exegesis and focuses on the original forms of the texts, or sources and redactions, or individual pericopes (literary units) within the whole. The literary critic, on the other hand, assumes conscious artistry in the finished product of the Bible, no matter how many sources or redactors contributed to it. His approach is holistic. The difference here is analogous to that between secular literary scholars and critics. While the scholar may investigate Shakespeare's life, or his sources, or textual emendations in the plays, the critic--acknowledging and sometimes depending on the scholar's work--will approach the finished product, the play itself. Similarly, one who studies the Bible as literature will acknowledge and often depend on the work of scholars and theologians, but will complement their disciplines with a different perspective.

A Brief History of the Discipline

Though C. S. Lewis has claimed that our age invented the phrase "the Bible as literature" (see 3D.7), interest in this approach can be traced far back into history--perhaps even to the Bible itself. For example, Paul's famous distinction between the "letter" which kills and the "spirit" which gives life (2 Corinthians 3:6) became, under the influence of Augustine (3E.1), the basic justification for a traditional medieval approach to the Bible as allegory--a kind of literature.

In the Renaissance, more attention came to be paid to the style and power of biblical literature (see Baroway, 3E.2). This emphasis can be traced back to Longinus, whose one-sentence praise of the style of the Genesis Creation narrative (see 3E.11) may be the earliest extra-biblical example of a literary comment on the Bible. Among Renaissance writers, Sidney and Milton made brief but important references to the significance and impact of the Bible as literature (3E.21 and 3E.15, respectively).

It was the eighteenth century, however, which produced the first significant and extended literary analyses of the Bible. The pioneering study was the work of Bishop Robert Lowth, whose Lectures on the Sacred Poetry of the Hebrews (3E.12) examined many facets of Old Testament poetry and first noted the characteristic Hebrew use of

poetic parallelism as a principle of versification. Lowth's work was
followed by that of the German Johann Gottfried von Herder (3E.10),
whose spirited defense of the Old Testament as poetry heralded the
romantic criticism of the next century.

This romantic fascination with biblical literature echoed through
the nineteenth century in isolated praises of the power, style, and
beauty of biblical verses. Walt Whitman's comment epitomizes the
attitude: "Even to our Nineteenth Century here are the fountain heads
of song" (3E.24). Concurrently, this century saw the rise of the
"higher criticism"; its concern for authorship and history paved the
way for the major interests of biblical scholarship in our era. But
E. S. Shaffer has argued that even the earlier higher critics took a
more holistic approach and, in their concern for myth, treated much
of the Bible as literature (3E.20).

In the twentieth century, critics turned their attention to
genre, and many studies attempted to classify biblical literature
into the traditional categories of narrative, lyric, drama, folklore,
and the like. A pioneer in this approach was Richard Moulton, who
produced both a study and an anthology (3E.16 and 1B.22) emphasizing
the generic approach; he was followed by, among others, Arthur Culler,
J. H. Gardiner, William Sypherd, and Laura Wild (see their studies in
section 3F). The romantic attitude also continued, and it can be
seen even at mid-century in Mary Ellen Chase's series of books for
"the common reader" (see 3F.5, 5M.4, and 5Q.4), which contain state-
ments like "the best letters ever written are in the Bible, and St.
Paul is the author of them, a more vivid letter writer than even
Horace Walpole or Lord Chesterfield, largely because he had far more
important things than they to say." Frequently earlier twentieth-
century critics tried to separate literary from religious approaches
by claiming that, whatever else it may be, the Bible is also great
literature. Typical is this comment from the foreword to Kathleen
Innes' 1930 study, The Bible as Literature (3F.24): "Mrs. Innes has
kept strictly to her chosen path, and has avoided theological or
critical entanglements."

More recently, there has been a renewed interest in literary
analysis of the Bible on a number of fronts. Evangelical Christians
have taken to justifying and studying the aesthetic qualities of the
Bible without sacrificing their view of its sacredness; they have
found a literary spokesman in Leland Ryken. (See the Index for his
works and those of others listed below.) Erich Auerbach's now famous
studies of Genesis and Mark (5C.1 and 8E.1) sparked an interest in a
new critical approach concentrating on the biblical text and its in-
ternal nuances and suggestions. Essentially formalist studies have
been undertaken in increasing numbers by both literary critics
(Kenneth Gros Louis) and biblical scholars (Edwin Good), and occasionally even by that rare avis with advanced training in both fields
(David Robertson). The widespread contemporary interest in language
and semiology has produced a great number of structuralist approaches

Introduction

to the Bible, though these are being written more by biblical scholars (like Robert Funk, John Dominic Crossan, and Dan Via) than by literary critics. In fact, there seems to be some danger that scholars will maintain their somewhat narrow vision of what literary critics do; whereas they formerly associated such criticism almost exclusively with source analysis, they now tend to identify it only with structuralism. Perhaps the healthiest approach on the horizon is an eclectic one that tries to connect literary analyses of the Bible with studies of its religious values (see Rosenberg, 3D.11, and Wilder, 7I.4, for example) or with the more traditional schools of biblical criticism (see Petersen, 7E.8). This approach places the Bible as literature in its rightful place as a complement to--not a substitute for or antagonist toward--traditional scholarship.

The Bibliography: Selection and Arrangement

As this brief historical survey shows, the Bible as literature is a complex and sometimes confusing field, creating difficulties for a bibliography like this. Three major problems are these: the vast amount of material written annually on the Bible, the different senses in which biblical scholars and literary critics have understood terms like "literary criticism," and the difficulty--perhaps impossibility--of distinguishing literary studies from other biblical studies. For these reasons, this bibliography is selective and by no means exhaustive. It is designed as a starting place.

The basic principle of selection has been to include material cited as useful by professionals working on the Bible as literature as defined above. I have consulted books and articles clearly designed for literary specialists and have followed up their bibliographical entries. I have added material recommended by teachers and writers working in the field, most of whom are named in the acknowledgements below. I have also consulted a number of traditional bibliographical sources in both biblical and literary fields (see section 2A). The final product therefore contains literary studies, commentaries, reference works, and other material--but only if such material has proven useful (or, in the case of very recent work, seems likely to prove useful) to someone with literary interests.

The following limits apply. Chronologically, most of the material has been published or re-issued between 1950 and mid-1978. (In a number of cases, important earlier work has been included, especially in sections 3E and 3F.) All of the studies have been written in or translated into English. I have included major reference works; significant historical, theological, and scholarly background; books, articles, and dissertations by and/or for critics and teachers of literature; significant editions and translations of the Bible; studies on the style and history of the English Bible; and pedagogical material. I have excluded editions or translations of separate books or Testaments (unless they contain extensive commentary of significance for literature), books and articles emphasizing doctrinal

or other nonliterary concerns (unless they have been cited as particularly useful by professionals working on the Bible as literature),
studies on religion in public education, school system course guides,
material aimed at students below the secondary level, and (perhaps
most important) the vast amount of material on the Bible in Literature or the Bible and literature. Since the purpose of this guide
is to serve primarily as a reference tool and only indirectly as a
survey of the development of critical thought, I have listed only
the latest edition of each book, indicating previous editions (where
appropriate) in the annotation. Similarly, there is only one main
entry per article, with the annotation citing significant reprints.

Some suggestions on how to use the book may be in order. The
material is divided into chapters and sections, with items listed
alphabetically by author within the latter. (In a few cases, where
a work is much better known by title than by author, the title appears first in the entry--for example, The Dartmouth Bible, 1B.9.)
Chapter 1 lists significant editions of major recent translations of
the entire Bible, texts and abridgements designed for literary study,
comments on and reviews of the major English translations, and studies of the history of the Bible as a book, from the earliest manuscripts to contemporary versions. Chapter 2 contains major reference works, including bibliographical sources for those wishing to
pursue further study, and a list of the most useful journals pertinent to the field. Chapter 3 focuses on the whole Bible. It begins
with introductions to the major contemporary approaches of biblical
scholars, and includes recent arguments for and against a literary
approach, the history of the Bible as literature up to the twentieth
century, and pedagogical material. Chapters 4 and 7 list studies
surveying all or most of the Old Testament and New Testament, respectively. They include major scholarly introductions and commentaries,
and literary milieu (texts and studies of lesser-known works from
Israel and her neighbors providing a literary context for the Bible,
including biblical pseudepigrapha and New Testament Apocrypha).
Within chapters 3, 4, and 7, literary studies are subdivided according to basic approach: general studies are followed by those concentrating on narrative, poetry, myth and legend, structuralist analyses, and the like.

Chapters 5 and 8 treat, respectively, the individual books of
the Old and New Testaments. Here works of scholarship and literary
analysis are listed together (partly to reduce the number of sub-
sections in the volume, but also because here it is often harder to
distinguish one from the other). The annotations will indicate which
works are primarily literary and which scholarly. Following recent
tradition, Luke's Gospel and the Book of Acts are listed together in
section 8F. For the sake of clarity and convenience, the Epistles in
chapter 8 are divided into those which do and those which do not tra-
ditionally bear Paul's name; general studies of the Epistles are included with the latter. In so arranging the material, I have avoided
the complex and controversial question of genuine Pauline authorship.

Introduction

Finally, chapter 6 yokes together studies of the whole Apocrypha and of the individual apocryphal books, since there are so few of the latter. Individual apocryphal books are listed separately by title in the Index.

The books of the Bible, including the Apocrypha, are named as in traditional Protestant Bibles and are arranged in the order generally found there. (Thus Canticle of Canticles will be listed as Song of Songs, for example.) Items which were hard to classify, or which might have been classified in two or more sections, are listed where they seemed to me to fit best, with appropriate cross references.

The annotations attempt to present the scope and basic approach of longer works, and to abstract the main point(s) of shorter ones. Since certain kinds of biblical studies follow essentially the same format, instead of repeating almost identical annotation explanations, I will present a general description of these works here. Introductions to the Bible or any of its parts usually supply extensive historical, textual, theological, and scholarly background on the unit being covered and its major components. Commentaries supply some background but focus more on line-by-line or section-by-section explications; they often reprint a translation of the text in question. Handbooks are designed more for lay readers; they provide basic background, commentary, and often summaries of, the whole unit and its major parts. Dictionaries provide fairly lengthy explanations of people, places, and topics relating to the Bible; encyclopedias contain longer articles of a similar nature. Word books attempt to explain the original meanings of terms either from the Hebrew or Greek texts or from older translations (like the King James) where language may have become archaic.

A few other principles of annotation should be mentioned. Many biblical studies will naturally reflect denominational, doctrinal, or scholarly biases. Where possible, I have tried to indicate the basic perspective from which each item is written; however, readers should be alert to such matters and consider them when evaluating an item. Also, a few scholarly studies demand at least some familiarity with biblical Hebrew or Greek, and others assume certain rudimentary knowledge about a text or a methodology; I have identified such studies as "advanced."

A more important point involves confusion over the term "literary criticism." Since it means something different to biblical scholars (who use it to refer to either source analysis or, more recently, structuralism) than to secular critics, and since it is often used in the former sense in titles and quotations from scholarly works, I have avoided the term as a designation of the kind of literary approach defined earlier. To refer to this approach in the annotations, I have used either "literary analysis" or "Bible as literature." Thus, "literary criticism" in the annotations does not mean what literary critics generally do!

Introduction

The symbol * designates an item I have not personally seen. In no case does this apply to a main entry. The few items I have not seen are alternate editions cited in the annotations.

Finally, the annotations indicate which works contain bibliographies for those wishing to investigate a matter further. Cross references are given by item numbers, not pages. Thus, 2B.3 means chapter 2, section B, item 3. If no number follows the decimal, or if no letter appears, the entire section or chapter is being cited. Thus 3D means chapter 3, section D; 5 means chapter 5.

The Index is a single alphabetical listing of authors and topics, interfiled. As in the annotations, references are to item numbers, not pages. With few exceptions, names of major figures and events in the Bible are not listed in the Index; to find references to them, the reader should look under the title of the book(s) in which these figures or events appear. Thus the name "Abraham" is not listed, but information about Abraham will be found under "Genesis: The Patriarchs"--section 5C. Also, cross references listed at the beginning of a section in the text, or in the annotations, are not repeated in the Index. To pursue a topic fully, the reader should check the Index listings and follow up cross references in the text itself.

Acknowledgments

I would like to acknowledge the generous assistance I have received from a number of sources. Small grants from the Lilly Foundation, from Indiana State University Evansville's Foundation, and from the Division of Humanities of Indiana State University Evansville, enabled me to undertake necessary travel for research. The library staffs of Indiana State University Evansville, the University of Evansville, and especially Indiana University have been most cooperative; special thanks are due to the Inter-Library Loan office at IU. Many individuals gave me assistance and suggestions at various stages of the project, including Daryl Adrian, Roy Battenhouse, Eugene Etheridge, Northrop Frye, Kenneth Gros Louis, Donald Juel, Clarence Walhout, Harold Watts, and Jan Wojcik. Special thanks go to Jim Ackerman, Thayer Warshaw, and the staff and participants in the 1977 and 1978 Summer Institutes on Teaching the Bible as Literature at Indiana University. Of course, none of these generous people are accountable for any errors or deficiencies in the finished product.

The staff of G. K. Hall & Co. have been most cooperative and encouraging. Special thanks go to my field editor, Ronald Gottesman. I am indebted to Jan Greer for typing the manuscript. Finally, love and thanks to my wife, JoAnne Gottcent, who helped in proofreading and in many other often intangible ways.

1 Editions and Translations

1A.1   The Anchor Bible. William Foxwell Albright and David Noel
Freedman, General Editors. Garden City, New York: Doubleday,
1964-.
      A series of volumes, each containing an introduction, trans-
lation, and notes on a book or books of the Old Testament, New
Testament, and Apocrypha. Edited by different scholars.
"Aimed at the general reader . . . yet . . . written with the
most exacting standards of scholarship." A valuable reference
tool for literary analysis. See 4C.7; 5A.7; 5G.2; 5H.3;
5J.1-2; 5K.1; 5L.32; 5M.7; 5N.2; 5P.5; 5R.2; 5S.2; 5T.1;
5V.1; 6F.3-5; 8D.1; 8F.6; 8G.2; 8H.1, 3; 8I.1, 14; 8J.6.

1A.2   The Bible: An American Translation. Old Testament translated by J. M. Powis Smith, et al. New Testament translated
by Edgar J. Goodspeed. Chicago: University of Chicago Press,
1935. 1148 pp.
      The books of the Protestant Bible with no notes or supple-
mentary material. See 1C.29.

1A.3   COHEN, A. Soncino Books of the Bible. Fourteen volumes.
London: Soncino, 1945-1952.
      The Hebrew text of the Jewish Scriptures with English
translations, introductions, and commentary.

1A.4   Good News Bible: The Bible in Today's English Version. New
York: American Bible Society, 1976. 1449 pp.
      "A new translation . . . [which] attempts in this century
to set forth the Biblical content and message in standard,
everyday, natural . . . English." Contains Old and New Testaments (not Apocrypha), word list, New Testament passages quo-
ted from the Septuagint, chronology, maps. (The New Testament
appeared alone in 1966 as Good News for Modern Man.)

1A.5   The Holy Bible (Authorized King James Version). Self-
pronouncing Edition. A Meridian Book. New York: New American
Library, 1974. 1034 pp.

1A   Complete Bibles

> A paperback edition omitting the Apocrypha. Appendices in-
> clude articles on translation, archaeology, geography, and
> other study aids. See 1A.7, 20, 21.

1A.6   The Holy Bible: A Translation from the Latin Vulgate in the
Light of the Hebrew and Greek Originals. [Translated by Ronald
Knox.] London: Burns & Oates, 1955. 1217 pp.
> A translation for British Roman Catholics with the Apocry-
> pha interspersed amid the Old Testament. Maps. See 1C.29.

1A.7   The Holy Bible: King James Version: A Reference Edition
with the Apocrypha. New York: American Bible Society, n.d.
1311 pp.
> Study edition contains supplementary reference guides (in-
> cluding, in some copies, a concordance) and maps. See 1A.5,
> 20, 21.

1A.8   The Holy Bible: Revised Standard Version. New York: Thomas
Nelson & Sons, 1952. 1302 pp.
> An American revision of the King James Version containing
> both Testaments but no Apocrypha. Several other editions of
> this translation are in print. The *Revised Standard Version
> of the Apocrypha is available in a separate volume, 1957. See
> 1A.9, 19.

1A.9   The Holy Bible: Revised Standard Version Containing the Old
and New Testaments with the Apocrypha-Deuterocanonical Books.
An Ecumenical Edition. New York: Collins, 1973. 1324 pp.
> Called "The Common Bible." Approved for use by both Roman
> Catholic and Protestant churches. Apocrypha and deuterocanon-
> ical books printed separately between the Testaments. Textual
> notes. See 1A.8, 19.

1A.10   The Holy Scriptures According to the Masoretic Text. Philadelphia: Jewish Publication Society of America, 1917. 1150 pp.
> An English translation of the Hebrew Scriptures by and for
> Jews, reflecting the traditional arrangement of the books into
> Law, Prophets, and Writings.

1A.11   The Jerusalem Bible. Alexander Jones, General Editor.
Garden City, New York: Doubleday, 1966. 2071 pp.
> A Roman Catholic translation based on a French version,
> compared with the Hebrew and Greek originals. Introductions,
> notes, auxiliary materials, and maps. A Reader's Edition
> (1968) with fewer trappings is available.

1A.12   JEWISH PUBLICATION SOCIETY OF AMERICA. [A New Translation
of Scripture.] Philadelphia: Jewish Publication Society of
America, 1967-.

2

A new English translation based on the Masoretic text. The
Torah appeared in 1967 and other volumes have been published
or will be published until the entire Hebrew Bible is complete.

1A.13   The Living Bible: Paraphrased. Wheaton, Illinois: Tyndale
House Publishers, 1971. 1020 pp.
   A compilation of earlier paraphrases of selected books.
The books of both Testaments are paraphrased--not translated--
into modern English.

1A.14   MOFFATT, JAMES. A New Translation of the Bible: Containing
the Old and New Testaments. New York: Harper & Row, 1922.1371 pp.
   A translation from the original Hebrew and Greek by a British biblical scholar.

1A.15   The New American Bible. Translated from the Original
Languages with Critical Use of All the Ancient Sources by
Members of the Catholic Biblical Association of America. New
York: P. J. Kenedy & Sons, 1970. 1811 pp.
   A Roman Catholic translation based on the original texts
instead of the Vulgate. Introductions and notes to each book
acknowledge critical/historical scholarship. Deuterocanonical
books interspersed throughout the Old Testament. Supplements
include the Dogmatic Constitution on Divine Revelation (from
Vatican II), a glossary of biblical theology terms, a survey
of biblical geography, and maps.

1A.16   New Catholic Edition of the Holy Bible. New York: Catholic
Book Publishing Company, 1957. 1553 pp.
   The Old Testament (including the deuterocanonical books) is
a compilation of the Douay and Confraternity of Christian Doctrine translations. The New Testament is in the CCD translation (a revision of the Challoner-Rheims Version edited by
Catholic scholars). Ancillary material and illustrations.

1A.17   The New English Bible with the Apocrypha. New York: Oxford
University Press, 1971. 1815 pp.
   A new British translation in modern idiom based on the ori-
ginal texts (i.e., not a revision of the King James Version).
Apocryphal books in separate section. Textual notes, but no
interpretive notes. See 1A.18.

1A.18   The New English Bible with the Apocrypha. Oxford Study Edi-
tion. Edited by Samuel Sandmel, M. Jack Suggs, and Arnold J.
Tkacik. New York: Oxford University Press, 1976. 1742 pp.
   Introductions to each book, explanatory notes, and an appen-
ded section, "Special Articles," which includes an essay on
"Literary Forms of the Bible." Maps.

Editions and Translations

1A Complete Bibles

1A.19   The New Oxford Annotated Bible with the Apocrypha: Revised Standard Version. Edited by Herbert G. May and Bruce M. Metzger. New York: Oxford University Press, 1973. 1951 pp.
    Includes the second edition of the Revised Standard Version New Testament. Notes, introductions, supplementary essays, and maps. See 1A.8-9.

1A.20   SCOFIELD, C. I., ed. The New Scofield Reference Bible. New edition edited by E. Schuyler English. New York: Oxford University Press, 1967. 1616 pp.
    A revision of a work first published in 1909. The King James Version with notes and auxiliary materials. The editors adhere "to the authority of the infallible Word of God in respect to both faith and practice." Concordance and maps. See 1A.5, 7, 21.

1A.21   WEIGLE, LUTHER A., ed. The New Testament Octapla: Eight English Versions of the New Testament in the Tyndale-King James Tradition. New York: Thomas Nelson & Sons, n.d. 1507 pp.
    Comparative translations side-by-side: Tyndale, Great Bible, Geneva Bible, Bishops' Bible, Rheims, King James, Revised Version, Revised Standard Version.

1B Textbooks for Literary Study

See also 4I.12.

1B.1   ABBOTT, WALTER M., ARTHUR GILBERT, ROLFE LANIER HUNT, and J. CARTER SWAIM, eds. The Bible Reader: An Interfaith Interpretation. New York: Bruce Publishing Company, 1969. 1019 pp.
    An ecumenically prepared anthology of selections from both Testaments and the Apocrypha with extensive notes and ancillary material. Selections chosen to give educated lay readers a better understanding of the Bible as a key to their culture. See 3M.1.

1B.2   ACKERMAN, JAMES S., and THAYER S. WARSHAW, with JOHN SWEET. The Bible as/in Literature. Glenview, Illinois: Scott, Foresman, 1976. 447 pp.
    A textbook designed for secondary schools, containing excerpts from the Revised Standard Version and selected literary pieces influenced by the Bible. Includes questions for close reading and for discussion, and suggested activities, marginal notes, and color photographs. A teacher's resource book is available.

1B.3   BALLOU, ROBERT O., ed. The Living Bible: A Shortened Version for Modern Readers Based on the King James Translation.
New York: Viking Press, 1952. 747 pp.
         Rearranged according to literary types. Includes a compo-
site gospel story of Jesus and selections from the nonscrip-
tural Logoi (sayings attributed to Jesus in pre-Gospel texts).
No chapter or verse divisions. Not to be confused with the
recent paraphrase bearing the same title (1A.13).

1B.4   BALLOU, ROBERT O., FRIEDRICH SPIEGELBERG, and HORACE L.
FRIESS, eds. The Bible of the World. New York: Viking Press,
1939. 1436 pp.
         Excerpts from the sacred writings of eight major religions:
Hindu, Buddhist, Confucianist, Taoist, Zoroastrian, Jewish,
Christian, and Mohammedan. Bibliography. A paperback con-
densed version (World Bible, 1972) is available.

1B.5   BATES, ERNEST SUTHERLAND, ed. The Bible Designed to Be
Read as Literature. Two volumes. London: The Folio Society,
1957-1958. Volume 1, 541 pp; volume 2, 568 pp.
         Selections from both Testaments and the Apocrypha (mostly
from the King James Version). Rearranged, with brief introductions to each book. Poetry printed in verse form. Illustrations. A one-volume edition (*New York: Simon & Schuster,
1970) is called The Bible Designed to Be Read as Living Literature: The Old and the New Testaments in the King James Version
(cited in 1B.6). See 4E.20.

1B.6   BROWN, DOUGLAS C., ed. The Enduring Legacy: Biblical Dimensions in Modern Literature. Scribner Student Paperback,
No. 35. New York: Charles Scribner's Sons, 1975. 406 pp.
         An anthology with excerpts from the King James Bible fol-
lowed by samplings from modern literary works relating directly
to the biblical themes. Introductions to each section and
study questions are provided. Designed "to show how a better
understanding of modern literature can be brought about by
tracing its Biblical influences; and . . . to discover what
insights modern authors can lend to an appreciation of the
Biblical literature to which they allude." Illustrations and
bibliography.

1B.7   CAPPS, ALTON C. The Bible as Literature. New York: Mc-
Graw-Hill, 1971. 432 pp.
         A student text based on selections from the Revised Stan-
dard Version, with extensive commentary. Material arranged
according to literary types.

1B   Textbooks for Literary Study

1B.8   CHASE, MARY ELLEN, ed. Readings from the Bible. New York:
Macmillan, 1952. 431 pp.
     Selections from the King James Version, chosen and arranged
as a reproduction of the author's college course on the literature of the Bible. Contains no chapter or verse divisions.

1B.9   The Dartmouth Bible: An Abridgement of the King James Version, with Aids to Its Understanding as History and Literature,
and as a Source of Religious Experience. Edited by Roy B.
Chamberlin and Herman Feldman. Second edition. Boston:
Houghton Mifflin, 1961. 1309 pp.
     Selections from both Testaments and the Apocrypha, with
introductions, prefaces, notes, and annotated maps. A special
feature is "The Combined Gospels," an integrated text providing a continuous narrative of the life and teachings of Jesus.
Reading list.

1B.10   DAVIS, O. B. Introduction to Biblical Literature. Rochelle
Park, New Jersey: Hayden Book Company, 1976. 245 pp.
     A textbook for literary students, containing excerpts from
the Old Testament only (King James Version), with brief introductions and questions for discussion.

1B.11   FRANK, JOSEPH, ed. Literature from the Bible. Boston:
Little, Brown, 1963. 413 pp.
     Selections from the King James Version. Each book or unit
is preceded by an introduction and a list of literary works
relevant to that part of the Bible. Poetry printed in verse
form.

1B.12   FRYE, ROLAND MUSHAT, ed. The Bible: Selections from the
King James Version for Study as Literature. Riverside Edition. Boston: Houghton Mifflin, 1965. 591 pp. (Later publication assumed by Princeton University Press.)
     A text containing about one-fourth of the Bible. Brief
introductions to each book. Poetry printed in verse form.
Bibliography, chronological outline, maps.

1B.13   GREENOUGH, RUTH HORNBLOWER, ed. The Home Bible: Arranged
for Family Reading from the King James Version, with Illustrations from Designs by William Blake. Two volumes bound
together. New York: Harper & Brothers, 1950. Part 1, 360 pp.;
part 2, 395 pp.
     Selections are rearranged and printed without citation of
book, chapter, or verse.

1B.14   HARRISON, G. B., ed. The Bible for Students of Literature
and Art. An Anchor Paperback. Garden City, New York:
Doubleday, 1964. 594 pp.

An abridgement of the King James Version including the Apocrypha. Includes an introduction and several brief appendixes explaining concepts like the Magi or Hebrew poetry. Maps.

1B.15   HARWELL, CHARLES W., and DANIEL MCDONALD, eds. <u>The Bible:</u> <u>A Literary Survey</u>. Indianapolis: Bobbs-Merrill, 1975. 305 pp.
An anthology with selections from both Testaments and the Apocrypha (King James Version). Introductions discuss the literary dimensions of the narratives. Illustrations, notes, and glossary.

1B.16   JACOBS, ROBERT G. <u>The Literature of the Bible</u>. Dubuque, Iowa: William C. Brown, 1969. 441 pp.
A text containing selections from the King James Version with introductory essays and notes. Poetry printed in verse form. "The discussions are devoted to defining and examining the literary forms which were employed by the Bible's many contributors." List of parallel readings (literary works reflecting biblical themes). Bibliography.

1B.17   LEE, ALVIN A., and HOPE ARNOTT LEE. <u>The Garden and the</u> <u>Wilderness</u>. Literature: Uses of the Imagination. Edited by Northrop Frye and W. T. Jewkes. New York: Harcourt Brace Jovanovich, 1973. 336 pp.
A text for high school students. "An anthology of selected Biblical writings combined with nonbiblical literary selections." Covers the Pentateuch. Illustrations and teachers manual. <u>See</u> 1B.18-19.

1B.18   LEE, ALVIN A., and HOPE ARNOTT LEE. <u>The Peaceable Kingdom</u>. Literature: Uses of the Imagination. Edited by Northrop Frye and W. T. Jewkes. New York: Harcourt Brace Jovanovich, 1974. 318 pp.
Sequel to 1B.17. Covers the New Testament. Illustrations and teachers manual.

1B.19   LEE, ALVIN A., and HOPE ARNOTT LEE. <u>The Temple and the</u> <u>Ruin</u>. Literature: Uses of the Imagination. Edited by Northrop Frye and W. T. Jewkes. New York: Harcourt Brace Jovanovich, 1973. 334 pp.
Sequel to 1B.17. Covers the Prophets and the Writings. Illustrations and teachers manual.

1B.20   <u>Literature from the Old Testament: Selections from the King</u> <u>James Version</u>. Boston: Houghton Mifflin, 1971. 318 pp.
An anthology with introduction by Mary Ellen Chase and drawings by Rembrandt. Suggestions for reading and discussion.

Editions and Translations

1B   Textbooks for Literary Study

1B.21   <u>The Mentor Bible: A Literary Abridgement</u>. Edited and with
          commentary by Michael Fixler. New York: New American Library,
          1973. 448 pp.
               An abridgement of the King James Version omitting chapter
          and verse numbers. Includes a composite arrangement of the
          four Gospels. Bibliography includes a section on the Bible
          as literature.

1B.22.   MOULTON, RICHARD G., ed. <u>The Modern Reader's Bible: The</u>
          <u>Books of the Bible with Three Books of the Apocrypha, Presented</u>
          <u>in Modern Literary Form</u>. New York: Macmillan, 1926. 1747 pp.
               The Revised Version, arranged and printed to suggest the
          literary structure of the Bible. Thus, poetry is printed in
          verse form, dramatic passages in dialogue, etc. Introductions
          and notes. Though now out of date, this book is interesting
          for an historical perspective on literary approaches to the
          Bible.

1C   <u>Style in the English Bible</u>

<u>See also</u> 1D; 3D.7, 12; 3F.5, 23, 45.

1C.1   ALLEN, WARD SYKES. "The Influence of Greek Rhetorical
          Structure on the English of the Authorized Version of the New
          Testament." Ph.D. dissertation, Vanderbilt University, 1963.
          Abstracted in <u>Dissertation Abstracts</u>, 24 (1963), 2010.
               Argues that the Greek text "governed the form of the English
          prose structure in the translation of the Authorized Version."

1C.2   BLUHM, HEINZ. "Literary Quality of Luther's Septembertesta-
          ment." <u>PMLA</u>, 81 (1966), 327-333.
               An analysis of Luther's translation of Galatians. Luther's
          New Testament heavily influenced sixteenth-century English
          versions of the Bible.

1C.3   CANBY, HENRY SEIDEL. "A Sermon on Style." <u>Saturday Review</u>
          <u>of Literature</u> (22 December 1928), pp. 533-535.
               The power of the English Bible was largely due to "the
          power of English eloquence, to style in the truest sense of
          the word." That power is now waning. Reprinted in 1C.17,
          pp. 23-28.

1C.4   CLARK, ELEANOR GRACE. "Must It Be King James?" <u>Catholic</u>
          <u>World</u>, 171 (1950), 192-197.
               A defense of the Roman Catholic Douay-Challoner Version
          over the King James, by a professor of English.

1C.5   COOK, ALBERT S. The Bible and English Prose Style: Selections and Comments. Boston: D. C. Heath, 1892. 131 pp.
A nineteenth-century work commenting on the Bible's style and its influence on English. Reprints excerpts from various commentators and a series of biblical selections from the King James Version for illustration.

1C.6   COOPER, LANE. Certain Rhythms in the English Bible: With Illustrations from the Psalms, Ecclesiastes, and the Lord's Prayer. Ithaca, New York: Cornell University Press, 1952. 16 pp.
A pamphlet analyzing anapestic and dactylic feet in the King James Version.

1C.7   DAICHES, DAVID. "Translating the Hebrew Bible," in his Literary Essays. Edinburgh: Oliver & Boyd, 1956, pp. 191-205.
Each translation, including the King James Version, produces a Bible different from the Hebrew original as well as from other translations. Compares various translations in English and other languages.

1C.8   DIERICKX, J. "Attitudes in Translation: Some Linguistic Features of the Jerusalem Bible." English Studies, 50 (1969), 10-20.
A review of this translation, including some observations on its stylistic value.

1C.9   ELIOT, T. S. "A Scholar Finds the Beauty Wrung Out of New English Bible's Verses." London Sunday Telegraph (16 December 1962), p. 7.
A scathing attack on the style and appropriateness of the New English Bible. Reprinted in 1C.17, pp. 54-57.

1C.10   EPPSTEIN, VICTOR. "The New English Bible of 1970." Midstream, 16, no. 8 (October 1970), 50-66.
A lengthy, mildly favorable review of the New English Bible.

1C.11   EVANS, BERGEN. "'Thou Shalt Not' or "You Shall Not.'" New York Times Magazine (26 March 1961), pp. 38, 72, 75-76, 78.
Questions whether the modern prose of newer translations (such as the New English Bible) really makes the Bible "more meaningful" than the poetic archaism of the King James Version.

1C.12   EVANS, BERGEN, ·and CORNELIA EVANS. [Biblical English.] In A Dictionary of Contemporary American Usage. New York: Random House, 1957, pp. 61-62.

1C Style in the English Bible

A brief note on the literary impact and significance of the King James Version. Reprinted in 1C.17, pp. 29-30.

1C.13   FREIMARCK, VINCENT. "The Bible and Neo-Classical Views of Style." Journal of English and Germanic Philology, 51 (1952), 507-526.
Surveys eighteenth-century critical views of the literary style of the Bible.

1C.14   HORNSBY, SAMUEL. "A Note on the Punctuation in the Authorized Version of the English Bible." English Studies, 54 (1973), 566-568.
The importance of punctuation in determining the meaning of a passage.

1C.15   HORNSBY, SAMUEL. "Style in the Bible: A Bibliography." Style, 7 (1973), 349-374.
An extensive annotated bibliography on the style of English translations of the Bible.

1C.16   HYMAN, STANLEY EDGAR. "'Understanded of the People,'" in his Standards: A Chronicle of Books for Our Time. New York: Horizon Press, 1966, pp. 7-11.
Acknowledges the greater clarity of the New English Bible, but argues that this translation is lacking in majesty and mystery, among other things. Reprinted in 1C.17, pp. 58-60.

1C.17   KEHL, D. G., ed. Literary Style of the Old Bible and the New. Bobbs-Merrill Series in Composition and Rhetoric. Indianapolis: Bobbs-Merrill, 1970. 64 pp.
An anthology of essays by various writers discussing the style of the King James Version and/or more modern translations. Bibliography. See 1C.3, 9, 12, 16, 19-21, 23, 26-27, 34.

1C.18   KNOX, R. A. On English Translation. The Romanes Lecture, 11 June 1957. Oxford: Clarendon Press, 1957. 26 pp.
Raises questions about the nature and effect of the King James Version.

1C.19   LOWES, JOHN LIVINGSTON. "The Noblest Monument of English Prose," in his Essays in Appreciation. Port Washington, New York: Kennikat Press, 1967, pp. 3-31.
Reprint of a collection of essays first published in 1936 (Boston: Houghton Mifflin). An essay in praise of the King James Version. Peculiar linguistic and historical circumstances made Jacobean English an almost ideal medium for capturing the beauty and simplicity of the original. Reprinted in 1C.17, pp. 8-17.

1C Style in the English Bible

1C.20   LUCAS, F. L. "The Greek 'Word' Was Different." <u>Saturday</u>
<u>Review of Literature</u> (1 April 1961), pp. 12-14.
A generally negative review of the New English Bible. Reprinted in 1C.17, pp. 50-53.

1C.21   MACDONALD, DWIGHT. "The Bible in Modern Undress." <u>The New</u>
<u>Yorker</u> (14 November 1953), pp. 168-192.
A brief history of the English Bible followed by a review
of the Revised Standard Version. Concludes that this version
is flatter, generally less powerful than the King James. Reprinted in 1C.17, pp. 33-43.

1C.22   MANSON, T. W. "The Revised Standard Version of the Bible."
<u>The Listener</u>, 49 (1953), 176-178.
Comments on the continual need for new Bible translations,
followed by a favorable review of this version.

1C.23   MAUGHAM, W. SOMERSET. <u>The Summing Up</u>. Garden City, New
York: Doubleday, 1938, pp. 33-36.
In this passage, Maugham argues that the King James Bible
had a harmful effect on English style because it encouraged
"the tendency to luxuriance" instead of simplicity. Reprinted
in 1C.17, pp. 31-32.

1C.24   MAVEETY, STANLEY ROSWELL. "A Study of the Style of the
King James and of the Rheims-Douay Translations of the Bible:
An Illustration of the Literary Consequences of Different
Theories of Translation." Ph.D. dissertation, Stanford University, 1956. Abstracted in <u>Dissertation Abstracts</u>, 16
(1956), 1250.
Contrasts Catholic and Protestant theories of translation
in the sixteenth and seventeenth centuries and their effects
on the style of these two Bibles.

1C.25   MAXWELL, J. C. "Designed to Be Read as the Bible."
<u>Spectator</u>, 6925 (17 March 1961), p. 370.
Favorable review of the New English Bible New Testament.

1C.26   MURRY, J. MIDDLETON. "The English Bible and the Grand
Style," in his <u>The Problem of Style</u>. New York: Oxford University Press, 1922, pp. 122-143.
Challenges the accepted notion of "the infallibility of the
style of the English Bible." The style varies in quality from
book to book. "It seems to me scarcely an exaggeration to say
that the style of one half of the English Bible is atrocious."
Excerpt reprinted in 1C.17, pp. 18-22.

1C.27   PRITCHETT, V. S. "The Finalised Version." <u>New Statesman</u>
(17 March 1961), pp. 425-426.

1C   Style in the English Bible

        A review of the New English Bible criticizing its blandness.
        Reprinted in 1C.17, pp. 61-63.

1C.28   RAUBER, D. F. "Regii Sanguisis Clamor ad Coelum: The Con-
         dition of Modern Biblical Translation." Catholic Biblical
         Quarterly, 32 (1970), 25-40.
         An article by a self-acknowledged "student of literature"
         arguing that the King James Bible is a more faithful rendering
         of the original than most modern translations because it tried
         to preserve the parallelism, connotations, and other literary
         effects of language. Modern translators are, ironically, too
         deeply immersed in a scholarship that emphasizes only the ra-
         tional, not the literary, power of words.

1C.29   RAYSOR, CECILY. "A Comparison of the Style of Four Recent
         Translations of the New Testament with That of the King James
         Version." Journal of Religion, 41 (1961), 73-90.
         The Revised Standard Version (1A.8), the Knox translation
         (1A.6), Goodspeed's "American Translation" (1A.2), and J. B.
         Phillips' "New Testament in Modern English." Compares only
         the English style of each, concluding that while there are
         definite differences, "the basic text holds up very well in
         all of them."

1C.30   SAINTSBURY, GEORGE. "The Authorized Version of the Bible,"
         in A Saintsbury Miscellany: Selections from His Essays and
         Scrapbooks. New York: Oxford University Press, 1947, pp. 124-
         131.
         Defends the style of the King James Version against attack-
         ers. "Here are the best words of the best period of English
         in the best order." Reprinted in 3F.33, pp. 178-184.

1C.31   SCHWARZ, W. Principles and Problems of Biblical Transla-
         tion: Some Reformation Controversies and Their Background.
         Cambridge: Cambridge University Press, 1955. 239 pp.
         A study of the conflict between different principles of
         biblical translation in the Renaissance, with particular atten-
         tion to the philological view of Erasmus versus the inspira-
         tional view of Luther. Bibliography.

1C.32   SKILTON, JOHN HAMILTON. "The Translation of the New Testa-
         ment into English, 1881-1950: Studies in Languages and Style."
         Ph.D. dissertation, University of Pennsylvania, 1961. Ab-
         stracted in Dissertation Abstracts, 22 (1961), 1187-1188.
         A stylistic study of English versions of the period. Con-
         cludes that most translations have not been entirely success-
         ful in achieving two major aims: to render the New Testament
         into modern, "everyday" English, and to revise the King James
         (or some other) version.

1C.33   TEMPEST, NORTON R. The Rhythm of English Prose: A Manual
for Students. Philadelphia: Folcroft Library Editions, 1972.
148 pp., passim.
    Reprint of a 1930 work. Observations on rhythm, prose
rhythm, and cadence, with some applications. Often cites the
King James Version for illustration. Bibliography.

1C.34   THOMPSON, DOROTHY. "The Old Bible and the New." Ladies
Home Journal (March 1953), pp. 11, 14, 203-206.
    A review of the Revised Standard Version. Concludes that it
is "weaker, less vivid, defective in imagery, less beautiful,
and less inspired" than the King James Version. Reprinted in
1C.17, pp. 44-49.

1C.35   WIKGREN, ALLEN PAUL. "A Critique of the Revised Standard
Version of the New Testament," in The Study of the Bible Today
and Tomorrow. Edited by Harold R. Willoughby. Chicago: University of Chicago Press, 1951, pp. 383-400.
    A favorable review. Despite some problems, this transla-
tion "represents a significant step in the achievement of the
most accurate English text and in the emancipation of the English Bible from the fetters of archaism."

1C.36   WILLEY, BASIL. "On Translating the Bible into Modern English." Essays and Studies, New Series 23 (1970), 1-17.
    Presents a justification for rendering the Bible into
"modern" speech, with particular reference to the New English
Bible New Testament. Recounts some of the discussion among
members of the literary panel for that edition. "Those who
talk of 'loss' . . . should make very certain that they themselves, in responding to the A.V., have not mistaken a sort of
liturgical trance for true understanding and spiritual
discernment."

1C.37   WILLS, GARRY. "Water in the Wine." National Review, 10
(1961), 284-285.
    A mixed review of the New English Bible New Testament.

1D History of Translations

See also 1A.21; 1C.21; 3B.4, 9; 3F.5, 16, 20, 31, 37; 4C.5.

1D.1   ALLEN, WARD, trans. and ed. Translating for King James:
Notes Made by a Translator of King James's Bible. Nashville:
Vanderbilt University Press, 1961. 167 pp.
    A reproduction of the notes of John Bois covering the
translation of Romans through Revelation. Photographs of the

1D   History of Translations

originals with translations on facing pages. Supplementary
essays on Bois and his work.

1D.2   AMERICAN BIBLE SOCIETY. A Ready-Reference History of the
English Bible. New York: American Bible Society, 1971. 49 pp.
A pamphlet tracing the history from the earliest English
versions to 1971. Bibliography.

1D.3   BRUCE, F. F. The English Bible: A History of Translations
from the Earliest English Versions to the New English Bible.
Revised edition. New York: Oxford University Press, 1970.
277 pp.
"Traces the history of the English Bible from its first beginnings in the seventh century up to the present time."

1D.4   BULLOUGH, SEBASTIAN. "English Versions since 1611," in
3B.3, pp. 162-168.
An account of some of the lesser-known English translations
that have appeared since the seventeenth century.

1D.5   BUSH, DOUGLAS. English Literature in the Earlier Seven-
teenth Century 1600-1660. Second edition, revised. The Ox-
ford History of English Literature, Vol. 5. Oxford: Clarendon
Press, 1962. 690 pp., passim.
Contains an account of the origin and nature of the King
James Bible (pp. 65-73).

1D.6   BUTTERWORTH, CHARLES C. The Literary Lineage of the King
James Bible, 1340-1611. Philadelphia: University of Pennsylvania Press, 1941. 406 pp.
The classic study of the development of the literary style
of the King James Bible. Surveys earlier English translations
and their influence on the King James. Bibliography. Reprinted: *New York: Octagon Books, 1971 (cited in 1C.15).

1D.7   The Cambridge History of the Bible. Edited by P. R. Ackroyd
and C. F. Evans (volume 1), G. W. H. Lampe (volume 2), and
S. L. Greenslade (volume 3). Three volumes. Cambridge:
Cambridge University Press, 1963-1970.
Articles by different scholars covering the history of the
Bible from the beginnings to the present day. Volume 1 car-
ries the story up to Jerome, volume 2 from the Church Fathers
to the Reformation, and volume 3 from the Reformation to the
present. "We have tried to give . . . an account of the text
and versions of the Bible used in the West, of its multiplica-
tion in manuscript and print, and its circulation; of attitudes
toward its authority and exegesis; and of its place in the life
of the Western Church." Bibliographies.

1D.8   CLARK, KENNETH WILLIS. "Ancient Books and the Biblical
Texts," in <u>Medieval and Renaissance Studies: Proceedings of
the Southeastern Institute of Medieval and Renaissance Studies,
Summer, 1968</u>. Edited by John L. Lievsay. Durham, North Caro-
lina: Duke University Press, 1970, pp. 21-37.
        A discussion of the role played by language and text in
understanding religious literature and a brief textual history of the Bible.

1D.9   COGGAN, DONALD. <u>The English Bible</u>. Writers and Their Work,
No. 154, edited by Bonamy Dobree. London: Longmans, Green,
1963. 43 pp.
        A brief discourse on the history of the English Bible by
the Archbishop of York. Select bibliography.

1D.10   CROOK, MARGARET B., ed. <u>The Bible and Its Literary Associa-
tions</u>. New York: Abindgon Press, 1937. 395 pp.
        An anthology of essays by members of various departments at
Smith College. Part 1 traces the history of the Bible from
its beginnings to the seventeenth century. Part 2 presents
three essays on the Bible's influence on Scottish and English
literature. Bibliography.

1D.11   DAICHES, DAVID. <u>The King James Version of the English
Bible: An Account of the Development and Sources of the English Bible of 1611 with Special Reference to the Hebrew Tra-
dition</u>. Chicago: University of Chicago Press, 1941. 236 pp.
        A brief history of the English Bible from 1523 to 1611 is
followed by studies of "the sources, equipment, and methods
of the translators."

1D.12   DEANESLY, MARGARET. <u>The Lollard Bible and Other Medieval
Versions</u>. Cambridge Studies in Medieval Life and Thought,
Vol. 1. Cambridge: Cambridge University Press, 1920. 503 pp.
        Studies "the history of mediaeval translations of the Vul-
gate, their place in the social history of the time, and the
attitude of authority towards them."

1D.13   DRIVER, G. R. "The Revised Version," in 3B.3, pp. 149-161.
        The stories behind, and brief commentaries on, the British
Revised Version of 1881-1885 and the earlier sections of the
American Revised Standard Version of 1952.

1D.14   FROST, STANLEY BRICE. "The English Bible," in <u>A Light unto
My Path: Old Testament Studies in Honor of Jacob M. Myers</u>.
Edited by Howard N. Bream, Ralph D. Heim, and Carey A. Moore.
Philadelphia: Temple University Press, 1974, pp. 205-221.

1D   History of Translations

Surveys the history of English versions from Caedmon's Hymn until the late nineteenth century and compares the styles of the major translations of the last century. "Splendid and remarkable as the new versions are, none of them has all the virtues; they can all gain immeasurably from each other."

1D.15   "The Geneva Bible." By a special correspondent of the Times [London]. In 3B.3, pp. 132–139.
A brief account of this important Puritan Bible which had great influence on the King James Bible.

1D.16   GRANT, FREDERICK CLIFTON. Translating the Bible. Greenwich, Connecticut: Seabury Press, 1961. 190 pp.
Covers translating from the development of the Hebrew Bible, through the Greek and Latin versions, to the New English Bible. Concluding chapter on principles and problems of translation. Bibliography.

1D.17   HERBERT, A. S. Historical Catalogue of Printed Editions of the English Bible 1525–1961. New York: American Bible Society, 1968. 580 pp.
"Revised and Expanded from the Edition of T. H. Darlow and H. F. Moule, 1903." A descriptive list of printed English Bibles, from Tyndale's New Testament (1525) to the New English Bible New Testament (1961). Appendixes cover commentaries with new translations and versions in English provincial dialects. Selected bibliography.

1D.18   HERKLOTS, H. G. G. How Our Bible Came to Us: A Literary Pilgrimage. London: Ernest Benn, 1954. 174 pp.
First published as Back to the Bible. Traces the ancestry of modern Bibles back to the earliest texts. Bibliography.

1D.19   HILLS, MARGARET T. The English Bible in America: A Bibliography of Editions of the Bible and the New Testament Published in America 1777–1957. New York: American Bible Society and the New York Public Library, 1961. 515 pp.
A descriptive bibliography of English Bibles published in America, including their locations. Includes an introductory essay on the history of the English Bible in this country. Bibliography.

1D.20   HUNT, GEOFFREY. About the New English Bible. London: Oxford University Press; Cambridge: Cambridge University Press, 1970. 91 pp.
A short treatise presenting the story behind this translation and explaining some of its features. Illustrations.

1D.21   KARPMAN, DAHLIA M.   "William Tyndale's Response to the Hebraic Tradition."   Studies in the Renaissance, 14 (1967),
110–130.
　　　Tyndale responded favorably to Hebrew biblical scholarship
in his translation, setting a new stamp of authority on it.

1D.22   KENYON, FREDERIC.   Our Bible and the Ancient Manuscripts.
Revised by A. W. Adams.   Fifth edition.   London: Eyre &
Spottiswoode, 1958.   352 pp.
　　　The history of the Bible as a book, from the earliest manu-
scripts to the English versions of the mid-twentieth century.

1D.23   LEWIS, C. S.   English Literature in the Sixteenth Century,
Excluding Drama.   The Oxford History of English Literature,
Vol. 3.   Oxford: Clarendon Press, 1954.   704 pp., passim.
　　　Contains a brief history of English translations of the
Bible in the sixteenth century and some observations on the
indebtedness of the King James Version to earlier translations.
Also notes Lewis' belief in the limited influence of the King
James Bible on later language and letters.   See especially
pp. 204–215.

1D.24   LUPTON, LEWIS.   A History of the Geneva Bible.   Eight vol-
umes.   London: Fauconberg Press, 1966–1976.
　　　The story behind the sixteenth-century Puritan translation.
Illustrations.

1D.25   MACGREGOR, GEDDES.   The Bible in the Making.   London: John
Murray, 1959.   310 pp.
　　　The development of the Bible from the writing of its books
to the English versions of the mid-twentieth century.

1D.26   MACGREGOR, GEDDES.   A Literary History of the Bible: From
the Middle Ages to the Present Day.   Nashville: Abingdon
Press, 1968.   400 pp.
　　　The history and nature of the major versions of the Bible
(mostly in English), starting with the early Middle Ages,
through the important translations of the sixteenth and seventeenth centuries and down to the New English Bible New Testament.   "Designed for the intelligent general reader, including
the college undergraduate."

1D.27   MAY, HERBERT GORDON.   Our English Bible in the Making: The
Word of Life in Living Language.   Philadelphia: Westminster
Press, 1952.   154 pp.
　　　A history of the English Bible from the first translations
through the Revised Standard Version.

1D History of Translations

1D.28   MOZLEY, J. F. Coverdale and His Bibles. London: Lutter-
worth Press, 1953. 369 pp.
     The life of Miles Coverdale and the stories behind the
Coverdale Bible, the Matthew Bible, and the Great Bible.

1D.29   MOZLEY, J. F. "The English Bible before the Authorized
Version," in 3B.3, pp. 127-131.
     A brief account of the history of the Bible in English be-
fore King James.

1D.30   MOZLEY, J. F. William Tyndale. New York: Macmillan, 1937.
376 pp.
     A biography of the translator of the first printed Bible in
English.

1D.31   MURRAY, GILBERT. "An Ancient Traditional Book," in his The
Rise of the Greek Epic. Fourth edition. London: Oxford Uni-
versity Press, 1934, pp. 93-119, passim.
     Discusses the nature of a book in early times using the
Hebrew Scriptures as an example.

1D.32   PARTRIDGE, A. C. English Biblical Translation. The Language Library. London: Andre Deutsch, 1973. 256 pp.
     Surveys English versions of the Bible from Anglo-Saxon
times to the era of the New English Bible and the Jerusalem
Bible. Of particular interest is the unusual attention given
to translations before the sixteenth century and between King
James and the late nineteenth century. Bibliography.

1D.33   POLLARD, ALFRED W., ed. Records of the English Bible: The
Documents Relating to the Translation and Publication of the
Bible in English, 1525-1611. Dawsons of Pall Mall, 1974.
399 pp.
     Reprint of a 1911 work. An introduction surveying the
Bibles of the period is followed by an extensive collection of
documents relating to the production of English versions from
Tyndale to King James. Includes the seldom reprinted preface
to the King James Version, "The Translators to the Reader"
(pp. 340-377).

1D.34   PRICE, IRA MAURICE. The Ancestry of Our English Bible: An
Account of Manuscripts, Texts, and Versions of the Bible.
Ninth edition. New York: Harper & Brothers, 1934. 374 pp.
     A history of the Bible from the earliest manuscripts to the
English versions of the early twentieth century. Particularly
complete coverage of manuscripts from ancient and medieval
times that predate English Bibles. Illustrations and
bibliography.

Editions and Translations

1D.35   REUMANN, JOHN. Four Centuries of the English Bible. Philadelphia: Muhlenberg Press, 1961. 76 pp.
A brief history of the English bible, emphasizing the significant translations from Wycliffe to the New English Bible.

1D.36   ROBERTS, B. J. "The Old Testament Hebrew Text," in 3B.3,
pp. 22-27.
A brief account of the textual history of the Old Testament.

1D.37   ROBINSON, H[ENRY] WHEELER, ed. The Bible in Its Ancient
and English Versions. Oxford: Clarendon Press, 1954. 349 pp.
Essays by different scholars on selected ancient biblical
versions and important English translations through the early
twentieth century. Bibliography.

1D.38   RYPINS, STANLEY. The Book of Thirty Centuries: An Introduc-
tion to Modern Study of the Bible. New York: Macmillan, 1951.
438 pp.
A study of the early texts of the Bible, up to and including
English translations, with a concluding introduction to the
"Higher Criticism."

1D.39   STRACHAN, JAMES. Early Bible Illustrations: A Short Study
Based on Some Fifteenth and Early Sixteenth Century Printed
Texts. Cambridge: Cambridge University Press, 1957. 178 pp.
Surveys the history of Bible translation into European
languages from c. 1450-1550. Reproduces, describes, and ex-
plains many of their illustrations. Bibliography.

1D.40   SYKES, NORMAN. "The Authorized Version of 1611," in 3B.3,
pp. 140-148.
An account of the origin of the King James Bible.

1D.41   TASKER, R. V. G. "The Manuscripts and Ancient Versions of
the New Testament," in 3B.3, pp. 94-98.
A brief introduction to the textual history of the New
Testament.

1D.42   THOMPSON, CRAIG R. The Bible in English 1525-1611. Folger
Booklets on Tudor and Stuart Civilization. Washington: Folger
Shakespeare Library, 1958. 37 pp.
A brief survey of the history of Bibles used in England
from the Vulgate through King James. Suggested reading list.
Illustrations.

1D.43   WEGENER, G. S. 6000 Years of the Bible. Translated by
Margaret Shenfield. New York: Harper & Row, 1963. 352 pp.

1D   History of Translations

> Begins with a brief survey of historical backgrounds of
> early biblical times and traces the origin and development of
> the Bible from its earliest stories, through the many trans-
> lations from ancient to modern times, to the Dead Sea Scrolls
> in the twentieth century. For the general reader.
> Illustrations.

1D.44   WEIGLE, LUTHER A. The English New Testament from Tyndale
to the Revised Standard Version. New York: Abingdon-Cokesbury
Press, 1949. 158 pp.
A survey of some of the problems involved in efforts to
translate the New Testament during the sixteenth through the
twentieth centuries. Bibliography.

1D.45   WILLIAMS, C. H. William Tyndale. London: Nelson, 1969.
191 pp.
A more recent biography of the sixteenth-century translator, superseding Mozley (See 1D.30). Bibliography.

1D.46   WILLOUGHBY, EDWIN ELIOTT. The Making of the King James
Bible: A Monograph, with Comparisons from the Bishops Bible
and the Manuscript Annotations of 1602. Los Angeles: Plantin
Press, 1956. 31 pp.
Briefly traces the story of the King James Bible from the
invention of the printing press until the book's appearance
in 1611. Illustrations include reproductions of pages from
the original edition.

2 General Reference Works

2A Bibliographical Sources

See also 1C.15; 2B; 3M.17.

2A.1   Bibliographic Index: A Cumulative Bibliography of Biblio-
         graphies. New York: H. W. Wilson. Bound annually.
             Lists books and longer articles that have bibliographies.
         See "The Bible as Literature" and related headings.

2A.2   Elenchus Bibliographicus Biblicus. Rome: Biblical Insti-
         tute Press. Published annually with the periodical Biblica
         until 1968; subsequent volumes bound separately.
             An annual bibliography listing all work on the Bible (and
         the parts thereof) done in the world during a given year.
         Editorial matter in Latin; titles and information about en-
         tries in original languages.

2A.3   Humanities Index. New York: H. W. Wilson. Bound annually.
         (Formerly the Social Sciences and Humanities Index; before
         that the International Index of Periodicals.)
             Entries are listed under "The Bible as Literature."

2A.4   MHRA Annual Bibliography of English Language and Litera-
         ture. London: Modern Humanities Research Association. Pub-
         lished annually.
             Entries tend to focus on the English Bible: its style, his-
         tory of translation, etc. See the index under "Bible."

2A.5   MLA International Bibliography. New York: Modern Language
         Association. Published annually.
             Since 1969 some material on the Bible as literature has
         been scattered among the entries listed under "Literature:
         General and Comparative: General Literature."

2A.6   Reader's Guide to Periodical Literature. New York: H. W.
         Wilson. Bound annually.
             Lists entries in more popular (as opposed to scholarly)
         periodicals. See "The Bible as Literature" and related
         headings.

2A Bibliographical Sources

2A.7   The Year's Work in English Studies. London: English Associ-
        ation. Published annually.
            Entries tend to focus on the English Bible: its style, his-
        tory of translation, etc. See the index under "Bible."

2B Useful Journals

2B.1   Christianity and Literature. Published quarterly by the
        Conference on Christianity and Literature. (Formerly the
        Conference on Christianity and Literature Newsletter.)
            Occasionally includes articles and book reviews on the
        Bible as literature. Each issue contains an annotated biblio-
        graphy which sometimes includes material on the Bible as
        literature (under "General"). A subject index, including a
        section on the Bible as literature, will soon be published as
        a supplement to the journal.

2B.2   Journal of Biblical Literature. Published quarterly by the
        Society of Biblical Literature.
            Focuses primarily on biblical scholarship, but often con-
        tains material useful for a study of the Bible as literature.

2B.3   Semeia: An Experimental Journal for Biblical Criticism.
        Published by the Society of Biblical Literature on an irregu-
        lar basis as material becomes available.
            Invites "studies employing the methods, models, and find-
        ings of linguistics, folklore studies, contemporary literary
        criticism," etc. Probably the most useful periodical for
        literary analyses of the Bible.

2B.4   Semitics. A monograph published annually as a subseries of
        Miscellanea of the University of South Africa.
            Contains useful articles (some advanced), many on rhetoric
        in the Bible.

2B.5   Soundings: An Interdisciplinary Journal. Published quar-
        terly by the Society for Values in Higher Education and Van-
        derbilt University.
            Occasionally includes articles on the Bible as literature.

2C Archaeological Background

See also 1A.5; 2G.4; 3B.3-4; 4A.19.

2C.1   ALBRIGHT, WILLIAM FOXWELL. Archaeology and the Religion of
        Israel: The Ayer Lectures of the Colgate-Rochester Divinity

School, 1941. Fourth edition. Baltimore: Johns Hopkins
Press, 1956. 258 pp.
   Five lectures on archaeology and the developing religions
of Israel and her Near Eastern neighbors.

2C.2   ALBRIGHT, WILLIAM FOXWELL. The Archaeology of Palestine.
Revised edition. Baltimore: Penguin Books, 1960. 271 pp.
   A study of the history and culture of ancient Palestine as
revealed by archaeology. Bibliography.

2C.3   BURROWS, MILLAR. What Mean These Stones? The Significance
of Archeology for Biblical Studies. New Haven: American
Schools of Oriental Research, 1941. 322 pp.
   A teacher of biblical history, literature, and theology explains the ramifications of archaeology for the studies of
text, languages, and dates of composition of the biblical
books, and other aspects of biblical background. Written from
"a liberal Protestant Christian" viewpoint. Bibliography.

2C.4   FINEGAN, JACK. Light from the Ancient Past: The Archeo-
logical Background of Judaism and Christianity. Second edition. Princeton: Princeton University Press, 1959. 676 pp.
   A history of Bible lands from about 5000 B.C. to about
A.D. 500, based on archaeological findings. Illustrations
and maps.

2C.5   FRANK, HARRY THOMAS. Bible Archaeology and Faith. Nashville: Abingdon Press, 1971. 352 pp.
   An introductory text explaining the general nature of biblical archaeology and surveying the history of Old and New
Testament times through archaeological evidence. Maps and
illustrations.

2C.6   GLUECK, NELSON. Rivers in the Desert: The Exploration of
the Negev, An Adventure in Archaeology. London: Weidenfeld &
Nicolson, 1959. 318 pp.
   A study of archaeological discoveries in the desert area
just south of Palestine. Maps and illustrations.

2C.7   ROWLEY, H[AROLD] H. From Joseph to Joshua: Biblical Tradi-
tions in the Light of Archaeology. London: Oxford University
Press, 1951. 214 pp.
   Background on the historical chronology of the Exodus and
settlement of Canaan, based on archaeological findings.
Bibliography.

2C.8   WILLIAMS, WALTER G. Archaeology in Biblical Research. New
York: Abingdon Press, 1965. 223 pp.

2C Archaeological Background

> Surveys the general nature of archaeology and the essence
> of biblical archaeology and relates archaeological insights
> about the biblical world. Bibliography.

2C.9 WRIGHT, G[EORGE] ERNEST. Biblical Archaeology. Second
edition. Philadelphia: Westminster Press, 1962. 291 pp.
"Summarizes the archaeological discoveries which directly
illumine biblical history, in order that the Bible's setting
in the ancient world . . . may be more readily comprehended."
Text and photographs show the historical development of biblical lands.

2C.10 WRIGHT, G[EORGE] ERNEST, EDWARD F. CAMPBELL, JR., and D. N.
FREEDMAN. The Biblical Archaeologist Reader. Three volumes.
Garden City, New York: Doubleday, 1961–1970.
Collection of articles by different scholars, originally
in the journal The Biblical Archaeologist. Background on recent archaeological discoveries shedding light on various
parts of the Bible. Illustrations. Volumes 1 and 2 reprinted
by Scholar's Press (University of Montana, Missoula), 1975.

2D Atlases and Geographical Background

See also 1A.5, 15.

2D.1 AHARONI, YOHANAN, and MICHAEL AVI-YONAH. The Macmillan
Bible Atlas. New York: Macmillan, 1968. 184 pp.
"The purpose of the Atlas is to show, as far as possible
through maps of each event, the changes and historical pro-
cesses in the lands of the Bible." Maps and text begin with
"The Four Winds of the Heavens and Their Names" and continue
through Old and New Testament periods to "The Church in the
Second Century A.D."

2D.2 BALY, DENIS, and A. D. TUSHINGHAM. Atlas of the Biblical
World. New York: World Publishing Company, 1971. 221 pp.
Text, pictures, maps, and drawings present a picture of the
wider Middle Eastern world and the smaller Palestine within it.

2D.3 GROLLENBERG, L. H. Atlas of the Bible. Translated and edited by Joyce H. Reid and H. H. Rowley. New York: Thomas Nelson & Sons, 1956. 166 pp.
Maps, photographs, and text trace the geographical development of Palestine through biblical times.

2D.4 KRAELING, EMIL G. Rand McNally Bible Atlas. Third edition.
Chicago: Rand McNally, 1966. 487 pp.
Text, pictures, drawings, and color maps tell the story of
the times and places referred to in the Bible.

2D.5   MAY, HERBERT G., ed. Oxford Bible Atlas. Second edition.
      London: Oxford University Press, 1974. 144 pp.
           Maps and accompanying text trace the historical develop-
      ment of Palestine through biblical times. Photographs.

2D.6   NEGENMAN, JAN H. New Atlas of the Bible. Edited by Harold
      H. Rowley. Translated by Hubert Hoskins and Richard Beckley.
      Garden City, New York: Doubleday, 1969. 208 pp.
           Text, photographs, drawings, and maps present the history
      and geography relevant to the Bible.

2D.7   PFEIFFER, CHARLES F., and HOWARD F. VOS. The Wycliffe His-
      torical Geography of Bible Lands. Chicago: Moody Press, 1967.
      624 pp.
           A one-volume survey of the history and geography of all
      Near Eastern and Mediterranean areas relevant to the Bible in-
      cluding those outside Palestine. Illustrations and maps.

2D.8   WRIGHT, GEORGE ERNEST, and FLOYD VIVIAN FILSON. The West-
      minster Historical Atlas to the Bible. Revised edition.
      Philadelphia: Westminster Press, 1956. 130 pp.
           Articles, photographs, and maps arranged to show the his-
      torical evolution of the biblical lands.

2E Dictionaries and Encyclopedias

See also 1A.15; 2I.1.

2E.1   ALLMEN, J. -J. von, ed. A Companion to the Bible. Intro-
      duction by H. H. Rowley. Translated by P. J. Allcock, et al.
      New York: Oxford University Press, 1958. 479 pp.
           A translation of a French work, Vocabulaire Biblique (1954).
      A dictionary with longer articles focusing on "the major theo-
      logical terms and ideas found in the Bible."

2E.2   BUTTRICK, GEORGE ARTHUR, ed. The Interpreter's Dictionary
      of the Bible: An Illustrated Encyclopedia. Four volumes. New
      York: Abingdon Press, 1962.
           Identifies and explains "all proper names and significant
      terms and subjects in the Holy Scriptures, including the Apoc-
      rypha, with attention to archaeological discoveries and re-
      searches into the life and faith of ancient times." Maps. A
      supplementary volume (1976), bringing the dictionary up to
      date, includes David Robertson's entry, "The Bible as Litera-
      ture" (pp. 547-551), which defines the field, surveys argu-
      ments for and against this approach, summarizes recent criti-
      cal stances (structuralist and nonstructuralist), and provides
      a bibliography. See 2H.5, 12.

General Reference Works

2E   Dictionaries and Encyclopedias

2E.3   CORNFELD, GAALYAHU, ed. Pictorial Biblical Encyclopedia: A
         Visual Guide to the Old and New Testaments. Tel Aviv: Hamikra
         Baolam Publishing House, 1964. 726 pp.
             An extensive reference listing names, places, and other
         items of biblical significance. Articles are accompanied by
         pictures and maps. Covers both Testaments and the Apocrypha.

2E.4   CROSS, F. L., and E. A. LIVINGSTONE, eds. The Oxford Dic-
         tionary of the Christian Church. Second edition. New York:
         Oxford University Press, 1974. 1550 pp.
             This comprehensive reference includes entries on the books
         of the Bible and other biblical subjects. Each article fol-
         lowed by a short bibliography.

2E.5   DAIGLE, RICHARD J., and FREDERICK R. LAPIDES. The Mentor
         Dictionary of Mythology and the Bible. New York: New American
         Library, 1973. 208 pp.
             Brief explanations of some of the major figures, places,
         and events of classical mythology and the Bible. Designed as
         an initial reference which may need to be complemented by more
         specialized volumes.

2E.6   DOUGLAS, J. D., et al. The New Bible Dictionary. Grand
         Rapids, Michigan: Wm. B. Eerdmans, 1962. 1423 pp.
             The product of an attempt "to stimulate evangelical bibli-
         cal scholarship." Illustrations and maps.

2E.7   The Family Bible Encyclopedia. Twenty-two volumes. New
         York: Curtis Books, 1972.
             An interdenominational encyclopedia for lay readers.
         Illustrations.

2E.8   GEHMAN, HENRY SNYDER, ed. The New Westminster Dictionary
         of the Bible. Philadelphia: Westminster Press, 1970. 1038 pp.
             Includes illustrations and color maps.

2E.9   HASTINGS, JAMES, ed. Dictionary of the Bible. Revised edi-
         tion by Frederick C. Grant and H. H. Rowley. New York:
         Charles Scribner's Sons, 1963. 1070 pp.
             A one-volume dictionary based on the Revised Standard Ver-
         sion, with cross references to other translations. Color
         maps.

2E.10   MCKENZIE, JOHN L. Dictionary of the Bible. New York:
         Bruce Publishing Company, 1965. 972 pp.
             A one-volume dictionary compiled entirely by this Roman
         Catholic priest. Illustrations.

2E.11   MILLER, MADELEINE S., and J. LANE MILLER. <u>Encyclopedia of</u>
<u>Bible Life</u>. Revised edition. New York: Harper & Brothers,
1955.   493 pp.
Articles on the lives and habits of the people of biblical
times.   Illustrations.

2E.12   MILLER, MADELEINE S., and J. LANE MILLER, eds. <u>Harper's</u>
<u>Bible Dictionary</u>. Revised by eminent authorities.   Eighth
edition.   New York: Harper & Row, 1973.   862 pp.
A one-volume dictionary originally published in 1952.
Includes many photographs, line drawings, and maps.

2E.13   RICHARDSON, ALAN, ed. <u>A Theological Word-Book of the Bible</u>.
New York: Macmillan, 1951.   290 pp.
A dictionary, with long entries by different scholars,
focusing on biblical words of theological significance.

2F   <u>Word Books</u>

<u>See also</u> 2G.3-4; 2I.1

2F.1   BARCLAY, WILLIAM. <u>New Testament Words</u>.   Philadelphia:
Westminster Press, 1974.   301 pp.
Lengthy articles explain the original meanings of sixty key
New Testament Greek words.   Includes all the words discussed
in Barclay's two previous volumes, *<u>A New Testament Wordbook</u>
and *<u>More New Testament Words</u>.

2F.2   BRIDGES, RONALD, and LUTHER A. WEIGLE. <u>The Bible Word</u>
<u>Book: Concerning Obsolete or Archaic Words in the King James</u>
<u>Version of the Bible</u>.   New York: Thomas Nelson & Sons, 1960.
432 pp.
Alphabetically arranged articles on 827 words and phrases
in the King James Version.   Explains the Renaissance meaning
of each and cites words or phrases substituted in more recent
translations.

2F.3   ELLIOTT, MELVIN E. <u>The Language of the King James Bible: A</u>
<u>Glossary Explaining Its Words and Expressions</u>.   Garden City,
New York: Doubleday, 1967.   239 pp.
Explains terms no longer in use and those which have changed
meaning since the seventeenth century.   Cites biblical verses
containing each term.   Bibliography.

2G   <u>Concordances</u>

<u>See also</u> 1A.7, 2O.

2G Concordances

2G.1   CRUDEN, ALEXANDER. <u>Cruden's Useful Concordance of the Holy</u>
<u>Scriptures: Comprising Most of the References Which Are Really</u>
<u>Needed</u>. Old Tappan, New Jersey: Fleming H. Revell, 1970.
352 pp.
        The classic concordance to the Old and New Testaments of
the King James Version. Originally published in 1737; available in many editions.

2G.2   ELLISON, JOHN W. <u>Nelson's Complete Concordance of the Re-</u>
<u>vised Standard Version Bible</u>. New York: Thomas Nelson & Sons,
1957. 2157 pp.
        The standard concordance to this version of the Bible, pro-
duced with the help of computers. Does not cite the Hebrew
and Greek words from which the English words were translated.

2G.3   STRONG, JAMES. <u>The Exhaustive Concordance of the Bible:</u>
<u>Showing Every Word of the Text of the Common English Version</u>
<u>of the Canonical Books, and Every Occurrence of Each Word in</u>
<u>Regular Order Together with a Comparative Concordance of the</u>
<u>Authorized and Revised Versions, Including the American Varia-</u>
<u>tions; also Brief Dictionaries of the Hebrew and Greek Words</u>
<u>of the Original, with References to the English Words</u>. New
York: Abingdon Press, 1955. 1808 pp.
        First published in 1890. Contains everything the subtitle
claims.

2G.4   YOUNG, ROBERT. <u>Analytical Concordance to the Bible</u>. Grand
Rapids, Michigan: Wm. B. Eerdmans, n.d. 1257 pp.
        Tells "<u>First</u>, What is the <u>original</u> Hebrew or Greek of any
ordinary word in [the] English Bible; <u>Second</u>, What is the
<u>literal</u> and primitive meaning of every such original word; and
<u>Third</u>, What are thoroughly true and reliable parallel pas-
sages." Based on the King James Version. Supplementary
material includes index-lexicons to the Old and New Testaments, a complete list of proper names in Scripture, and
chapters on recent discoveries in Bible lands (by William F.
Albright).

2H Commentaries and Handbooks

<u>See also</u> 1A.1, 3; 4C; 6C; 7C.

2H.1   ACKROYD, P. R., A. R. C. LEANEY, and J. W. PACKER, eds.
<u>The Cambridge Bible Commentary on the New English Bible</u>. Cam-
bridge: Cambridge University Press, 1963-.
        A series of volumes presenting the layman with background
and scholarship reflecting new developments that influenced

the New English Bible. Introductory volumes on each Testament
and the Apocrypha are followed by commentaries on the books of
the Bible. The New Testament series was completed in 1967;
the other series are in progress.

2H.2   ALEXANDER, DAVID, and PAT ALEXANDER, eds. Eerdman's Handbook to the Bible. Carmel, New York: Guideposts, 1973.
680 pp.
    An illustrated reference with background information on the
Bible in general and on each book of the Old and New Testaments. Indexes to key themes, people, parables, and related
matters.

2H.3   BLACK, MATTHEW, and H. H. ROWLEY, eds. Peake's Commentary
on the Bible. London: Thomas Nelson & Sons, 1962. 1141 pp.
    Revision of a classic work by A. S. Peake (1919). A one-
volume commentary. Designed to "convey with precision, and
yet in a popular and interesting way, the meaning of the original writers." General articles, introductory articles, and
commentaries on the individual books of both Testaments. Maps.

2H.4   BROWN, RAYMOND E., JOSEPH A. FITZMYER, and ROLAND E.
MURPHY. The Jerome Biblical Commentary. Two volumes (bound
together). Englewood Cliffs, New Jersey: Prentice-Hall, 1968.
Volume 1 (The Old Testament), 703 pp; volume 2 (The New Testament and Topical Articles), 889 pp.
    "A compact commentary on the whole Bible written by Roman
Catholic scholars according to the principles of modern Biblical criticism."

2H.5   BUTTRICK, GEORGE ARTHUR, ed. The Interpreter's Bible: The
Holy Scriptures in the King James and Revised Standard Versions, with General Articles and Introduction, Exegesis, Exposition for Each Book of the Bible. Twelve volumes. New
York: Abingdon Press, 1951-1957.
    The work of many scholars from different denominations,
this is probably the most thorough and valuable line-by-line
commentary on the whole Bible. See 2E.2; 2H.12.

2H.6   CLARKE, W. K. LOWTHER. Concise Bible Commentary. New
York: Macmillan, 1953. 1010 pp.
    A one-volume commentary based on the Revised Version.
Introductory articles, and section-by-section commentaries on
each book of the Bible including the Apocrypha. Maps and
illustrations.

2H.7   FULLER, REGINALD C., LEONARD JOHNSTON, and CONLETH KEARNS,
eds. A New Catholic Commentary on Holy Scripture. London:
Thomas Nelson & Sons, 1969. 1396 pp.

2H   Commentaries and Handbooks

A complete revision of the earlier A Catholic Commentary on Holy Scripture (1953) reflecting new developments in Catholic biblical scholarship resulting from Vatican II.   General articles and discussions of each book.   Maps.

2H.8   GRANT, FREDERICK C.   How to Read the Bible.   New York: Morehouse-Gorham, 1956.   168 pp.
Guidelines for Christian laymen reading both Testaments and the Apocrypha.   Bibliography.

2H.9   GUTHRIE, D., J. A. MOTYER, A. M. STIBBS, and D. J. WISEMAN. The New Bible Commentary: Revised.   Third edition.   Grand Rapids, Michigan: Wm. B. Eerdmans, 1970.   1325 pp.
A one-volume commentary containing general articles and individual treatments of each book of the Old and New Testaments. Treats the Bible by attempting to combine "unqualified belief in its divine inspiration, essential historical trustworthiness and positive Christian usefulness with careful scholarship."   Maps.

2H.10   HIERS, RICHARD H.   Reader's Guide to the Bible.   Nashville: Abingdon Press, 1978.   160 pp.
Brief introductions providing background and commentary on each biblical book including the Apocrypha.

2H.11   KELLY, BALMER H., DONALD G. MILLER, and ARNOLD B. RHODES, eds.   The Laymen's Bible Commentary.   Twenty-five volumes. Richmond, Virginia: John Knox Press, 1959-1964.
Commentaries by various scholars.   "Based on the conviction that the Bible has the Word of good news for the whole world." An introductory volume is followed by volumes dealing with one or more books.   Both Old and New Testaments are covered.

2H.12   LAYMON, CHARLES M., ed.   The Interpreter's One-Volume Commentary on the Bible.   Nashville: Abingdon Press, 1971. 1400 pp.
A companion to 2E.2 and 2H.5.   Introduction and commentary on each book of the Bible including the Apocrypha, with general articles, illustrations, and maps.

2H.13   NEIL, WILLIAM.   The Bible Story.   Nashville: Abingdon Press, 1971.   272 pp.
A guidebook for the general reader.   Interweaves a summary of and commentary on the biblical story from Genesis to Revelation.   Illustrations.

2H.14   NEIL, WILLIAM.   Harper's Bible Commentary.   New York: Harper & Row, 1962.   544 pp.

A short commentary for lay readers. "Based on the assumption that the biblical writers were primarily theologians,
. . . that the Old and New Testaments are part of one and the
same revelation. . . ."

2H.15   WRIGHT, G. ERNEST, and REGINALD H. FULLER. The Book of the
Acts of God: Christian Scholarship Interprets the Bible.
Garden City, New York: Doubleday, 1957. 372 pp.
    Introductory chapters provide an overview of the Bible and
how it came to be written, followed by discussions of each
part of both Testaments and the Apocrypha. Designed for
laymen.

2I Miscellaneous Reference Works

See also 3F.13.

2I.1   BULLINGER, E[THELBERT] W. Figures of Speech Used in the
Bible: Explained and Illustrated. Grand Rapids, Michigan:
Baker Book House, 1968. 1152 pp.
    Reprint of an 1898 work. Biblical verses are grouped and
classified according to the figure of speech (ellipsis, oxy-
moron, symbol, etc.) they illustrate.

2I.2   DEEN, EDITH. All of the Women of the Bible. New York:
Harper & Row, 1955. 432 pp.
    An exhaustive index with extended commentaries on the major
women. Bibliography.

2I.3   FREEMAN, JAMES M. Manners and Customs of the Bible. Plainfield, New Jersey: Logos International, 1972. 515 pp.
    Reprint of an older work. "The design of this volume is to
illustrate the Bible by an explanation of the Oriental customs
to which it refers." Material arranged by chapter and verse.

2I.4   MEAD, FRANK S. Handbook of Denominations in the United
States. New fifth edition. Nashville: Abingdon Press, 1970.
265 pp.
    A reference book describing the history, doctrine, organi-
zation, and present status of over 250 religious bodies in the
United States. Background on doctrinal views related to the
Bible.

2I.5   NAVE, ORVILLE J. Nave's Topical Bible: A Digest of the
Holy Scriptures. Chicago: Moody Press, 1970. 1464 pp.
    References to Scripture arranged under various topics and
subtopics.

3 The Bible as a Whole

3A <u>Scholarly Approaches to the Bible</u>

<u>See also</u> 1D.38; 3B.4; 4C.23; 5A.3; 5I.4; 5M.10-11, 28; 5Q.13; 5S.3;
8A.2-5, 8, 10-11; 8I.16.

3A.1   HABEL, NORMAN C. <u>Literary Criticism of the Old Testament</u>.
        Guides to Biblical Scholarship, Old Testament Series. Phila-
        delphia: Fortress Press, 1971. 96 pp.
            A brief introduction to "literary criticism" in the bibli-
        cal scholarship sense: a study of "the structure, style,
        forms, and sources of a document." Deals almost exclusively
        with source studies. Annotated bibliography.

3A.2   HAHN, HERBERT F. <u>The Old Testament in Modern Research</u>.
        Expanded edition. Philadelphia: Fortress Press, 1966. 344 pp.
            A survey of modern approaches to the interpretation of the
        Old Testament. Provides background and information about
        these approaches; does <u>not</u> include the Bible as literature.

3A.3   HAYES, JOHN H. <u>Old Testament Form Criticism</u>. Trinity Uni-
        versity Monograph Series in Religion, Vol. 2. San Antonio:
        Trinity University Press, 1974. 309 pp.
            An anthology of essays for the advanced student. Contains
        Martin J. Buss, "The Study of Forms"; Jay A. Wilcoxen, "Nar-
        rative"; W. Malcolm Clark, "Law"; W. Eugene March, "Prophecy";
        Erhard Gerstenberger, "Psalms"; and James L. Crenshaw,
        "Wisdom."

3A.4   JACKSON, JARED J., and MARTIN KESSLER, eds. <u>Rhetorical
        Criticism: Essays in Honor of James Muilenburg</u>. Pittsburgh
        Theological Monograph Series, No. 1. Pittsburgh: Pickwick
        Press, 1974. 305 pp.
            These essays apply the principles of rhetorical criticism
        (described in the introduction as a method "that requires
        attention to the text itself: its own integrity, its dramatic
        structure, and its stylistic features") to various biblical
        texts. Contents include: Martin Kessler, "Rhetorical Criti-
        cism of Genesis 7" (pp. 1-17); Isaac M. Kikawada, "The Shape

3A   Scholarly Approaches

of Genesis 11:1-9" (pp. 18-32); E. John Hamlin, "The Liberator's Ordeal: A Study of Exodus 4:1-9" (pp. 33-42); Ashley S. Rose, "The 'Principles' of Divine Election: Wisdom in 1 Samuel 16" (pp. 43-67); A. D. Ritterspach, "Rhetorical Criticism and the Song of Hannah" (pp. 68-74); George Ridout, "The Rape of Tamar" (pp. 75-84); Jared J. Jackson, "Style in Isaiah 28 and a Drinking Bout of the Gods (RS 24.258)" (pp. 85-98); Kiyoshi K. Sacon, "Isaiah 40:1-11: A Rhetorical-Critical Study" (pp. 99-116); Robert W. Fisher, "The Herald of Good News in Second Isaiah" (pp. 117-132); Fredrick Holmgren, "Yahweh the Avenger: Isaiah 63:1-6" (pp. 133-148); Walter Brueggeman, "Israel's Sense of Place in Jeremiah" (pp. 149-165); Thomas M. Raitt, "Jeremiah's Deliverance Message to Judah" (pp. 166-185); J. Kenneth Kuntz, "The Canonical Wisdom Psalms of Ancient Israel: Their Rhetorical, Thematic, and Formal Dimensions" (pp. 186-222).

3A.5   KESSLER, MARTIN. "A Methodological Setting for Rhetorical Criticism." Semitics, 4 (1974), 22-36.
Investigates the scope of rhetorical criticism, defined in terms of both classical and "new rhetoric" concerns, and argues that this is the best approach for coordinating the other critical stances on the Bible.

3A.6   KLEIN, RALPH W. Textual Criticism of the Old Testament: From the Septuagint to Qumran. Guides to Biblical Scholarship, Old Testament Series. Philadelphia: Fortress Press, 1974. 96 pp.
An introduction to the oldest branch of biblical scholarship, sometimes called "lower criticism." Explains the principles and problems involved in establishing the most reliable text of the Old Testament. Bibliography.

3A.7   KOCH, KLAUS. The Growth of the Biblical Tradition: The Form-Critical Method. Translated from the second German edition by S. M. Cupitt. New York: Charles Scribner's Sons, 1969. 248 pp.
An introduction to form criticism, primarily for theological students. Deals frequently with questions of literary types and literary criticism and contains an especially pertinent chapter on "Characteristics of Hebrew Poetry."

3A.8   KRENTZ, EDGAR. The Historical-Critical Method. Guides to Biblical Scholarship, Old Testament Series. Philadelphia: Fortress Press, 1975. 96 pp.
A brief general discussion of "the predominant method of biblical interpretation in use today." A good introduction to modern biblical scholarship.

3A.9   MCKNIGHT, EDGAR V. What is Form Criticism? Guides to Biblical Scholarship, New Testament Series. Philadelphia: Fortress Press, 1969. 96 pp.
          A brief account of the origins and nature of form criticism.
Glossary and bibliography.

3A.10   MONTGOMERY, ROBERT M. An Introduction to Source Analysis
of the Pentateuch. Auxiliary Studies in the Bible. Nashville:
Abingdon Press, 1971. 140 pp.
          A programmed learning text for college students treating
the theory that the Pentateuch is the work of at least four
different schools of thought.

3A.11   MUILENBURG, JAMES. "Form Criticism and Beyond." Journal
of Biblical Literature, 88 (1969), 1-18.
          An explanation and defense of rhetorical criticism, which
Muilenburg defines as a concern for the nature of Hebrew
literature: its structural patterns and the devices by which
it is unified.

3A.12   PERRIN, NORMAN. What is Redaction Criticism? Guides to
Biblical Scholarship, New Testament Series. Philadelphia:
Fortress Press, 1969. 96 pp.
          A brief account of the origins, nature, and implications of
this approach to the Bible. Glossary and bibliography.

3A.13   TUCKER, GENE M. Form Criticism of the Old Testament.
Guides to Biblical Scholarship, Old Testament Series. Philadelphia: Fortress Press, 1971, 96 pp.
          A brief explanation of the method and illustrations of its
application to narrative genres and prophetic literature.
Bibliography.

3B. Historical and Cultural Background

See also 1D.43; 2C; 2D; 2E.12; 2I.3; 3F.5, 37; 4A; 6A; 7A.

3B.1   ALBRIGHT, WILLIAM FOXWELL. From the Stone Age to Christianity: Monotheism and the Historical Process. Second edition.
An Anchor Book. Garden City, New York: Doubleday, 1957.
450 pp.
          The history of the ancient Near East as it relates to the
Bible, with special emphasis on the development of monotheism
in human civilization.

3B.2   BARON, SALO WITTMAYER. A Social and Religious History of
the Jews. Volumes 1-2. Second edition. New York: Columbia
University Press, 1952. Volume 1, 427 pp; volume 2, 493 pp.

3B History and Culture

Part of a series on the history of the Jews, these volumes focus on ancient times through the Talmudic period (c. A.D. 500).

3B.3 The Bible Today: Historical, Social, and Literary Aspects of the Old and New Testaments Described by Christian Scholars. New York: Harper & Brothers, 1955. 224 pp.

An anthology of articles by different scholars on many aspects of the Bible, several of literary significance, and others providing historical, archaeological, or theological background. An expansion of a Bible supplement originally published by the London Times (June 1954), See 1D.4, 13, 15, 29, 36, 40-41; 4C.13, 20, 26; 4J.2; 5Q.8; 6C.3; 8I.11.

3B.4 BRATTON, FRED GLADSTONE. A History of the Bible: An Introduction to the Historical Method. Boston: Beacon Press, 1959. 394 pp.

Includes archaeological backgrounds of the Old Testament, the making of the Old and New Testaments, the transmission of the Bible from Greek manuscripts to English translations, and a brief history of the higher criticism. Bibliography.

3B.5 DIMONT, MAX I. Jews, God and History. New York: Simon & Schuster, 1962. 464 pp.

A history of the Jews for the lay reader. The first three chapters (about one-third of the whole) provide historical background for the Bible. Bibliography.

3B.6 GUTHRIE, W. K. C. The Greeks and Their Gods. Boston: Beacon Press, 1955. 402 pp.

Religious and cultural background for the Hellenistic milieu of the late Old Testament, the Apocrypha, and the New Testament.

3B.7 KELLER, WERNER. The Bible as History: A Confirmation of the Book of Books. Translated by William Neil. New York: Bantam Books, 1956. 538 pp.

Uses modern scientific evidence to demonstrate to lay readers that much of the Bible may be based on historical fact. Covers both Testaments. Photographs and bibliography.

3B.8 KRAMER, SAMUEL NOAH. History Begins at Sumer. Garden City, New York: Doubleday, 1959. 272 pp.

Originally published as From the Tablets of Sumer: Twenty-Five Firsts in Man's Recorded History (1956). The story of twenty-seven historical "firsts" recorded on ancient tablets from Sumer. Many explicit biblical parallels, including "The First 'Moses,'" "The First 'Noah,'" and "The First Tale of Resurrection." Illustrations.

The Bible as a Whole

3B.9   MOULD, ELMER W. K. <u>Essentials of Bible History</u>. Revised
edition. New York: Ronald Press, 1951. 739 pp.
A textbook for the beginning student providing extensive
background on the political, historical, cultural, and literary
milieu of the Bible. Covers Old and New Testament periods and
traces the history of the Bible to the mid-twentieth century.
Bibliography, illustrations, and maps.

3B.10   NATIONAL GEOGRAPHIC SOCIETY. <u>Everyday Life in Bible Times</u>.
National Geographic Society, 1967. 448 pp.
A stunning collection of color photographs, drawings, and
text depict life in the biblical lands, as it was and as it is.
For the layman.

3B.11   NOTH, MARTIN. <u>The History of Israel</u>. Second edition.
Translated by P. R. Ackroyd. New York: Harper & Brothers,
1960. 499 pp.
Covers the period from about 1200 B.C. to the time of
Christ. Bibliography.

3B.12   SCHWARZ, LEO W., ed. <u>Great Ages and Ideas of the Jewish
People</u>. New York: Modern Library, 1956.
The first three sections (pp. 3-212) provide background on
the political and cultural history of the Jews through c.
A.D. 500. Bibliography.

3C <u>Scholarly and Theological Background</u>

See also 2C; 2E.13; 2H; 2I.4; 3B.1, 3; 4B; 6B; 7B.

3C.1   BRIGHT, JOHN <u>The Kingdom of God: The Biblical Concept and
Its Meaning for the Church</u>. New York: Abingdon-Cokesbury
Press, 1953. 288 pp.
Traces the development of the concept in the Bible and
emphasizes (from a Christian perspective) the relationship
between the two Testaments.

3C.2   CHARLES, R. H. <u>A Critical History of the Doctrine of a
Future Life in Israel, in Judaism, and in Christianity</u>. Re-
vised edition. London: Adam & Charles Black, 1913. 494 pp.
Traces the development of eschatological beliefs through
both Testaments. Reprinted as *<u>Eschatology</u> (New York:
Schocken Books, 1963).

3C.3   ROBINSON, JAMES M., and JOHN B. COBB, JR., eds. <u>The New
Hermeneutic</u>. New Frontiers in Theology, Vol. 2. New York:
Harper & Row, 1964. 255 pp.

3C Scholarly & Theological Background

A symposium with contributions from Continental and American theologians on the new role of language in biblical interpretation. Theological background on the relation of language, myth, and literary form to an understanding of the Bible.

3C.4   SUTCLIFFE, EDMUND F. <u>Providence and Suffering in the Old and New Testaments</u>. London: Thomas Nelson & Sons, 1953. 183 pp.

Surveys ancient nonbiblical views on the relationship between providence and suffering, and traces these themes through the Bible.

3D <u>The Bible as Literature: Arguments For and Against</u>

<u>See also</u> 2E.2; 3E; 3F.11; 3J.7, 9; 3M; 4E.20; 5D.6; 5H.8; 5I.6; 5X.5; 7E.8; 7I.4.

3D.1   ALTER, ROBERT. "A Literary Approach to the Bible." <u>Commentary</u>, 60 (December 1975), 70-77.

Decries the lack of good literary studies of the Bible, and offers a reading of the Tamar-Judah story (Genesis 38) as an illustration of a literary approach to biblical narrative. <u>See</u> letters in response in <u>Commentary</u>, 61 (March 1976), 14-20.

3D.2   BOONSTRA, HARRY. "Biblical Metaphor: More than Decoration." <u>Christianity Today</u>, 21 (1976), 346-347.

An evangelical justification for biblical metaphor. "God allowed the writers of Scripture to play seriously with language and make lively, at times even outlandish, comparisons."

3D.3   BROWN, SPENCER. "The Bible and a Liberal Education: Its Benefits, as Seen by an Unbeliever." <u>Commentary</u>, 16 (1953), 311-320.

An English teacher argues for the Bible as a "monument of literature and moral insight." <u>See</u> reply in <u>Commentary</u>, 16 (1953), 593.

3D.4   DODD, C. H. <u>The Authority of the Bible</u>. Revised edition. New York: Harper & Brothers, 1960. 288 pp.

This apologia assumes that "the Bible (or most of it) <u>is</u> great literature." Chapter 1, "Literature and Authority," justifies the Bible on the basis of the special genius of its writers.

3D.5   ELIOT, T. S. "Religion and Literature," in <u>Selected Prose of T. S. Eliot</u>. Edited by Frank Kermode. New York: Harcourt Brace Jovanovich, 1975, pp. 97-106, passim.

Includes observations on the Bible as literature. While it is possible to appreciate the literary merits of the Bible, those who enjoy it solely as literature are essentially parasites.

3D.6   GORDIS, ROBERT. "The Bible as a Cultural Monument." Chapter 15 of The Jews: Their History, Culture, and Religion. Third edition. Edited by Louis Finkelstein. Philadelphia: Jewish Publication Society of America, 1960, volume 1, pp. 783–822.
The significance of the Bible as a work of literature, religion, and history. Bibliography.

3D.7   LEWIS, C. S. The Literary Impact of the Authorised Version. The Ethel M. Wood Lecture Delivered before the University of London on 20 March 1950. London: Athlone Press, 1950.   26 pp.
Questions the supposed influence of the King James Version on English language and literature. Doubts that the Bible can be read "as literature" apart from an appreciation of its sacredness. Also published in the *Facet Book Series (Philadelphia: Fortress Press, 1967). Reprinted in They Asked for a Paper (London: Geoffrey Bles, 1962), pp. 26–50; Selected Literary Essays (Cambridge: Cambridge University Press, 1969), pp. 126–145; and 3F.33, pp. 343–362.

3D.8   MCCOWN, C. C. "Symbolic Interpretation." Journal of Biblical Literature, 63 (1944), 329–338.
Attacks modern allegorical and symbolic readings of the Bible. "The interpreter must seek to understand the language of the ancient writer as he himself meant it."

3D.9   MOLLENKOTT, VIRGINIA RAMEY. "Literary Approaches to the Bible: A Review Essay." Christianity and Literature, 25, no. 2 (1976), 47–52.
Reviews several books and includes an impassioned plea "for those of us who teach literature to become militant about the importance of literary approaches to biblical interpretation." Includes reviews of 3F.34, 40; 4E.25, 27; 7E.12, 15.

3D.10   QUILLER-COUCH, ARTHUR. "On Reading the Bible," in his On the Art of Reading. New York: G. P. Putnam's Sons, 1920, pp. 141–206.
Three lectures arguing that the English Bible is a literary work that should be included in academic programs of traditional literature. The last lecture discusses Job to illustrate the point.

3D   Arguments For and Against

3D.11   ROSENBERG, JOEL. "Meanings, Morals, and Mysteries: Literary Approaches to Torah." Response, 9, no. 2 (Summer 1975),
67-94.
           Argues that literature interprets humanity as much as vice
versa, and applies this idea to the Torah and the rabbinic
tradition. Calls for a new way of looking at the Bible as
literature: "the Bible's value as a religious document is in-
timately and inseparably related to its value as literature."

3D.12   RUDOLPH, ERWIN P. "Beauty in the Bible." Christianity
Today, 20 (1975), 251-252.
           An evangelical call to recognize the aesthetic and stylistic
value of biblical writing.

3D.13   RYKEN, LELAND. "A Christian Approach to Literature."
Christianity Today, 14 (1969), 218-220.
           An evangelical justification for literature which argues
that the Bible is literature and that reading of the Bible en-
courages the reading of literature.

3D.14   RYKEN, LELAND. "Good Reading in the Good Book." Christianity Today, 19 (1975), 368-371.
           Argues the validity of the Bible as literature for evange-
lical Christians.

3D.15   RYKEN, LELAND. "Literary Criticism of the Bible: Some
Fallacies," in 3F.22, pp. 24-40.
           Argues that literary analysis of the Bible is valid and
should be performed according to the principles of the secular
literary critic, not those of the biblical scholar. "A plea
for the recognition of the legitimacy of literary criticism,
performed by teachers of literature, as a doorway to the understanding and enjoyment of the Bible."

3E   The Bible as Literature: History of

See also 1B.22; 1C.13, 24, 31-32; 3F; 4E; 5Q.6; 7I.4.

3E.1   AUGUSTINE, SAINT. On Christian Doctrine. Translated by
D. W. Robertson, Jr. Library of Liberal Arts, No. 80. New
York: Liberal Arts Press, 1958. 191 pp., passim.
           A treatise on the interpretation of the Bible, completed in
A.D. 427. Of historical interest to literary people in that
it makes an early defense of an allegorical method of reading
Scripture with an explanation of the pleasure to be found in
"cracking" the allegory.

The Bible as a Whole

3E.2   BAROWAY, ISRAEL. "The Bible as Poetry in the English
        Renaissance: An Introduction." Journal of English and Germanic
        Philology, 32 (1933), 447-480.
            Argues that Renaissance critics were acutely aware of the
        Bible's value as literature and bequeathed this viewpoint to
        later generations. Surveys Renaissance commentary on the poe-
        tic nature of the Bible.

3E.3   BOECKH, AUGUST. On Interpretation and Criticism. Trans-
        lated and edited by John Paul Pritchard. Norman: University
        of Oklahoma Press, 1968. 193 pp., passim.
            An English translation of two sections of Boeckh's nine-
        teenth-century Encyclopaedie und Methodologie der philolo-
        gischen Wissenschaften. Useful for its general theory of
        literature and especially for its comments on the New Testa-
        ment in Part 2: Theory of Hermeneutics.

3E.4   FREI, HANS W. The Eclipse of Biblical Narrative: A Study
        in Eighteenth and Nineteenth Century Hermeneutics. New Haven:
        Yale University Press, 1974. 365 pp.
            Studies that period of biblical interpretation during
        which realistic and figurative interpretation broke down and
        was replaced by the "higher criticism." Background on the his-
        tory of the Bible as literature. See 3F.2; 3G.9.

3E.5   FREIMARCK, VINCENT. "Timothy Dwight's Dissertation on the
        Bible." American Literature, 24 (1952), 73-77.
            A note on Dwight's *Dissertation on the History, Eloquence,
        and Poetry of the Bible (1772), showing it to be an important
        eighteenth-century American contribution to the study of the
        Bible "purely as literature."

3E.6   FROEHLICH, KARLFRIED. "'Always to Keep the Literal Sense
        in Holy Scripture Means to Kill One's Soul': The State of Bib-
        lical Hermeneutics at the Beginning of the Fifteenth Century,"
        in Literary Uses of Typology from the Late Middle Ages to the
        Present. Edited by Earl Miner. Princeton: Princeton Uni-
        versity Press, 1977, pp. 20-48.
            A study of a medieval argument over whether the Bible should
        be interpreted literally or figuratively.

3E.7   GOETHE, JOHANN WOLFGANG VON. Poetry and Truth. Translated
        by Minna-Steele Smith. London: G. Bell and Sons, 1911.
            The first three parts of this autobiography contain com-
        ments on the appeal of the literary power of the Bible to
        young Goethe's imagination. See especially volume 1, pp. 110-
        111, 114-116, 120-122, 242-246, and volume 2, pp. 56-58. Ex-
        cerpts reprinted in 3F.33, pp. 165-174.

3E   History of

3E.8   GRANT, ROBERT M. A Short History of the Interpretation of
the Bible. Revised edition. New York: Macmillan, 1963.
224 pp.
     Covers Christian interpretation from Jesus' view of the Old
Testament, through medieval views of the whole Bible, to recent perspectives. Select English bibliography.

3E.9   HANSON, R. P. C. Allegory and Event: A Study of the Sour-
ces and Significance of Origen's Interpretation of Scripture.
Richmond, Virginia: John Knox Press, 1959. 400 pp.
     A study of the Early Christian tradition of reading the
Bible allegorically. Bibliography.

3E.10   HERDER, JOHANN GOTTFRIED VON. The Spirit of Hebrew Poetry.
Translated by James Marsh. Naperville, Illinois: Alec R.
Allenson, 1971. 614 pp.
     The first part of this important eighteenth-century state-
ment presents, in dialogue form, a defense of the Old Testament as poetry. Part two, in expository form, examines the
poems of the Old Testament through the time of David (i.e.,
the Psalms). Reprint of a nineteenth-century book. Excerpt
on Job (from Dialog IV) reprinted in 5L.9, pp. 141-156. Other
excerpts reprinted in 3F.33, pp. 133-165.

3E.11   LONGINUS. On Great Writing (On the Sublime). Translated
by G. M. A. Grube. New York: Liberal Arts Press, 1957, chapter 9, p. 14
     This classic treatise contains perhaps the earliest comment
on the Bible as literature in its brief praise of the style of
the opening lines of Genesis. Available in other editions and
translations.

3E.12   LOWTH, ROBERT. Lectures on the Sacred Poetry of the Hebrews. Two volumes. Translated by G. Gregory. New York:
Garland Publishing Company, 1971. Volume 1, 418 pp.; volume 2,
478 pp.
     Facsimile reproductions of the famous lectures in which the
eighteenth-century bishop first noted the poetic nature of
much biblical writing and first identified the characteristic
Hebrew use of poetic parallelism. Contains thirty-four lectures on aspects of many kinds of biblical poetry, from short
odes to longer works like Song of Songs and Job. Lectures 14
("Of the Sublime in General, and of Sublimity of Expression in
Particular") and 33 ("The Poem of Job Not a Perfect Drama")
reprinted in Eighteenth-Century Critical Essays. Edited by
Scott Elledge. Ithaca, New York: Cornell University Press,
1961, volume 2. Lecture 33 also reprinted in 5L.9, pp. 132-
140. Lecture 32 ("Of the Poem of Job") reprinted in 5L.19;
pp. 175-192.

3E.13   LYNCH, WILLIAM F.   Christ and Apollo: The Dimensions of the
Literary Imagination.   New York: Sheed & Ward, 1960.   285 pp.,
passim.
    This study of the relationship between the definite and the
abstract in literature includes a chapter ("The Christian
Imagination") on the fourfold medieval approach to the Bible:
the literal, tropological, analogical, and anagogical, and, in
a supplement, some documents relating to this approach.

3E.14   MÂLE, EMILE.   The Gothic Image: Religious Art in France of
the Thirteenth Century.   Translated by Dora Nussey.   New York:
Harper & Brothers, 1958.   441 pp., passim.
    Contains information about the history of symbolic and alle-
gorical interpretations of the Bible through the early Middle
Ages. (See especially Book 4, "The Mirror of History.")

3E.15   MILTON, JOHN.   "The Reason of Church Government Urged
against Prelaty," in John Milton: Complete Poems and Major
Prose.   Edited by Merritt Y. Hughes.   New York: Odyssey Press,
1957, pp. 667-671, passim.
    Milton compares himself and his mission to the ancient
Hebrew writers and justifies seeing parts of the Bible as
literature. Excerpt reprinted in 3F.33, pp. 125-127. Available in other anthologies.

3E.16   MOULTON, RICHARD G.   The Literary Study of the Bible.   Revised edition.   New York: AMS Press, 1970.   585 pp.
    Reprint of an 1899 work. An early consideration of the
Bible as a literary work. Discusses the various kinds of
literature (lyric poetry, epic, prophecy, etc.) found in the
Bible.

3E.17   PREUS, JAMES SAMUEL.   From Shadow to Promise: Old Testament
Interpretation from Augustine to the Young Luther.   Cambridge,
Massachusetts: Harvard University Press, Belknap Press, 1969.
313 pp.
    This study of Luther's indebtedness to biblical tradition
provides an extensive survey of the history of biblical interpretation in the Middle Ages and early Renaissance.
Bibliography.

3E.18   ROSTON, MURRAY.   Prophet and Poet: The Bible and the Growth
of Romanticism.   London: Faber & Faber, 1965.   204 pp.
    A study of the developing awareness of the Bible as a lite-
rary work in eighteenth-century England. The poetry of the
Old Testament provided a model for the emerging poets of pre-
romanticism. Considerable attention is given to the nature
of biblical poetry as it was seen in this age. Bibliography.

3E   History of

3E.19   SCHOLEM, GERSHOM G. On the Kabbalah and Its Symbolism.
New York: Schocken Books, 1965. 216 pp.
Background on the history of Jewish mystical interpretation
of Scripture (especially the Torah) and its relation to myth.

3E.20   SHAFFER, E. S. "Kubla Khan" and the Fall of Jerusalem: The
Mythological School in Biblical Criticism and Secular Literature 1770-1880. Cambridge: Cambridge University Press, 1975.
371 pp.
Studies the mythological school of German "Higher Criticism"
as it influenced England in the late eighteenth and nineteenth
centuries. Argues that early "Higher Criticism" saw the Bible
as literature. Includes Eichhorn's outline of the poetic action of Revelation (pp. 292-295). Bibliography.

3E.21   SIDNEY, SIR PHILIP. A Defense of Poetry. Edited by J. A.
Van Dorsten. London: Oxford University Press, 1966. 112 pp.
In this famous treatise Sidney argues that the psalms and
parables of the Bible may be seen as valuable literature. Excerpts reprinted in 3F.33, pp. 117-119. Available in other
editions and anthologies; also called "An Apology for Poetry"
or "A Defense of Poesy."

3E.22   SMALLEY, BERYL. The Study of the Bible in the Middle Ages.
Notre Dame, Indiana: University of Notre Dame Press, 1964.
428 pp.
Surveys the study of the Bible in medieval religious orders
and schools. Background on the medieval distinction between
the letter and the spirit in biblical interpretation.

3E.23   THOMPSON, FRANCIS. "Books that Have Influenced Me," in his
Literary Criticisms. Edited by Terence L. Connolly. New
York: E. P. Dutton, 1948, pp. 542-544.
Praises the poetry and gnomic wisdom of the Bible. Re-
printed in 3F.33, pp. 176-178.

3E.24   WHITMAN, WALT. "The Bible as Poetry." [From November
Boughs.] In The Works of Walt Whitman. Edited by Malcolm
Cowley. New York: Funk & Wagnalls, 1968, volume 2, pp. 396-
398.
Praises the power of the Bible's literature. "Even to our
Nineteenth Century here are the fountain heads of song."
Reprinted in 3F.33, pp. 174-176.

3F   The Bible as Literature: General Studies

See also 1A.18; 2E.10; 3K.5; 3M.12; 4E; 6E; 7E.

The Bible as a Whole

3F.1   ALTMANN, ALEXANDER, ed. Biblical Motifs: Origins and Trans-
formations. Cambridge, Massachusetts: Harvard University
Press, 1966. 251 pp.
An anthology of advanced studies of motifs in the Bible and
some later sources. Includes Cyrus H. Gordon, "Leviathan:
Symbol of Evil" (pp. 1-10); F. M. Cross, "The Divine Warrior
in Israel's Early Cult" (pp. 11-30); S. Talmon, "The 'Desert
Motif' in the Bible and in Qumran Literature" (pp. 31-64);
Michael C. Astour, "Political and Cosmic Symbolism in Genesis
14 and in Its Babylonian Sources" (pp. 65-112); David Neiman,
"The Date and Circumstances of the Cursing of Canaan" (pp. 113-
134); Judah Goldin, "The End of Ecclesiastes: Literal Exegesis
and Its Transformation" (pp. 135-158); and Nahum Glatzer, "The
Book of Job and Its Interpreters" (pp. 197-220, on views of
Job through the centuries).

3F.2   ARMERDING, CARL EDWIN, and W. WARD GASQUE. "Significant
Books of 1974: The Bible as a Whole." Christianity Today, 19
(1975), 563-564.
An excerpt from a lengthy annotated bibliography focusing
on the Bible as literature. Includes brief reviews of 3E.4;
3F.22, 34.

3F.3   ARMSTRONG, EDWARD A. The Folklore of Birds: An Enquiry
into the Origin and Distribution of Some Magico-Religious
Traditions. London: Collins, 1958. 286 pp., passim.
Includes occasional references to bird symbolism in the
Bible. Illustrations and bibliography.

3F.4   BECKER, JOHN E. "The Law, the Prophets, and Wisdom: On the
Functions of Literature." College English, 37, no. 3 (November 1975), 254-264.
An examination of the Bible and the kinds of literature it
contains, leading to "a discussion of the functions of literature within American culture."

3F.5   CHASE, MARY ELLEN. The Bible and the Common Reader. Revised edition. New York: Macmillan, 1952. 340 pp.
A literary commentary, designed for the lay reader, on
selected books from the Old and New Testaments and the Apocrypha. Introductory chapters consider the nature of the
Bible, the history and value of the King James Version, and
the history, racial, and literary characteristics of the
Hebrews. Reading list. See 4E.6.

3F.6   COPE, GILBERT. Symbolism in the Bible and the Church. New
York: Philosophical Library, 1959. 287 pp.

3F   General Studies

A study of the imagery and symbolism of the Bible and the
church from a twentieth-century perspective. Extensive treatment of myth and archetypal patterns.

3F.7   CULLER, ARTHUR J. Creative Religious Literature: A New
Literary Study of the Bible. New York: Macmillan, 1930.
356 pp.
A study of the Bible as literature organized around literary types and genres. Includes suggestions for comparing
biblical literature with other literature of the same theme
or type. Chapter bibliographies.

3F.8   DAVIDSON, GUSTAV. "The Named Angels in Scripture."
Cimarron Review (Oklahoma State University), 13 (1970), 65-69.
Finds a total of seven angels named in the Bible, several
of whom have significance for literature.

3F.9   DILLISTONE, F. W. Christianity and Symbolism. Philadel-
phia: Westminster Press, 1955. 320 pp.
Background on the nature of symbolism and its role in
Christianity. Bibliography.

3F.10   DINSMORE, CHARLES ALLEN. The English Bible as Literature.
Boston: Houghton Mifflin, 1931. 328 pp.
Part 1 studies the genius and discipline of the Hebrew
people as contributors to the literary greatness of the Bible
in its original languages and in English. Parts 2 and 3 survey the literary qualities of both Testaments, emphasizing
the overall effect of the Bible as a unity.

3F.11   DINSMORE, CHARLES ALLEN. "The Literary Qualities of the
English Bible," in Education for Christian Service, by Members
of the Faculty of the Divinity School of Yale University. New
Haven: Yale University Press, 1922, pp. 113-132.
An older essay arguing that the Bible is literature and
surveying its literary traits.

3F.12   ETHERIDGE, EUGENE W. The Bible as Literature. Cincinnati:
The Writer's Voice, 1975.
Three hour-long cassettes with accompanying workbook. Lec-
tures on the Bible as literature, prose of the Bible, and poe-
try of the Bible, adapted from Professor Etheridge's course at
Indiana State University. A conservative approach.

3F.13   FERGUSON, GEORGE. Signs and Symbols in Christian Art.
London: Oxford University Press, 1954. 191 pp.
Lists and explains the meaning of the most common tradi-
tional Christian signs and symbols. 350 illustrations.

3F.14   FORBES, CHERYL. "The Bible as Literature." Christianity
Today, 19 (1975), 652-653.
Includes favorable reviews of 3F.22, 34.

3F.15   FUNK, ROBERT W., ed. "Literary Critical Studies of Biblical Texts." Semeia, 8 (1977). 138 pp.
Special issue with articles on different parts of the Bible
as literature. See 5I.2, 9; 5M.21; 5Q.14; 6F.2; 8F.4.

3F.16   GARDINER, J. H. The Bible as English Literature. New York:
Charles Scribner's Sons, 1906. 413 pp.
An early literary study of the Bible based on a course
taught by the author in Harvard University's Department of
English. Arranged in literary units with chapters on: the
narrative, the poetry, the Wisdom Books, etc., and two final
chapters on the history of translation and the King James
Bible.

3F.17   GARDNER, HELEN. The Business of Criticism. Oxford: Clarendon Press, 1959.
The second section of this book, "The Limits of Literary
Criticism" (pp. 79-157; Riddle Memorial Lectures, 1956), argues the need for a historical approach to works of literature.
Dame Gardner, a renowned literary critic, focuses on a literary approach to the Bible for illustration, with particular
emphasis on the drunkenness of Noah and the poetry of Mark.

3F.18   GARRISON, WEBB B. [GARY WEBSTER, pseud.] Laughter in the
Bible. St. Louis: Bethany Press, 1960. 160 pp.
Surveys the nature and uses of laughter in the Bible.
Laughter is seen as a response to many human situations, in-
cluding "amusement, mirth, delight, satire, sarcasm, wit,
scorn, irony, and joy."

3F.19   GORDIS, ROBERT. "The Heptad as an Element of Biblical and
Rabbinic Style." Journal of Biblical Literature, 62 (1943),
17-26.
A study of the use of the number seven as a stylistic element in the Bible and rabbinic writings.

3F.20   GRIERSON, SIR HERBERT. "The English Bible," in Romance of
English Literature. Edited by W. J. Turner. New York: Hastings House, 1944, pp. 19-60.
A brief essay treating the translators from Wycliffe to
Moffatt, the Bible as literature (specifically the Bible's
influence on English writers), and the attitude of writers
from Milton to Ruskin toward the idea of the Bible as the word
of God. Photographs, some in color. Published in a separate
volume (London: Collins, 1947).

3F   General Studies

3F.21   GROS LOUIS, KENNETH R. R.   "Critical Pre-Suppositions in
Approaching the Bible as Literature."   Christianity and Literature, 24, no. 2 (Winter 1975), 42-44.
        Lists eleven presuppositions used by the author in approach-
ing the Bible as literature and applies some of them to the
narrative of David (1 Samuel 16 - 1 Kings 2).

3F.22   GROS LOUIS, KENNETH R. R., with JAMES S. ACKERMAN and
THAYER S. WARSHAW.   Literary Interpretations of Biblical Narratives.   Nashville: Abingdon Press, 1974.   352 pp.
        A collection of essays by scholars trained in literary cri-
ticism.   Most were originally presented as lectures at the Indiana University Summer Institute on Teaching the Bible as
Literature.   See 3D.15; 3F.2, 14; 4E.5; 5B.7-8; 5C.8; 5D.1-2;
5G.4; 5H.8; 5I.3; 5L.15; 5O.4; 5R.1; 5X.6; 8D.8; 8E.5; 8J.7.

3F.23   HENN, T. R.   The Bible as Literature.   New York: Oxford
University Press, 1970.   270 pp.
        Each chapter considers a literary aspect of the Bible such
as themes, languages, style, imagery, character, and action.
Bibliography.

3F.24   INNES, KATHLEEN E.   The Bible as Literature.   Philadelphia:
Folcroft Library Editions, 1975.   255 pp.
        Reprint of a 1930 work.   Readings of selected sections of
the Bible as literature.   Covers parts of both Testaments and
the Apocrypha.   The author "has kept strictly to her chosen
path, and has avoided theological or critical entanglements."

3F.25   JONES, HOWARD MUMFORD.   "The Bible from a Literary Point of
View," in Five Essays on the Bible: Papers Read at the 1960
Annual Meeting of the American Council of Learned Societies.
New York: American Council of Learned Societies, 1960, pp. 45-
59.
        A brief treatise on the literary qualities of the King
James Version.   "My mandate is to discuss the Bible as a work
susceptible of literary evaluation, not as an infallible
scripture, a quarry for proof texts, a source for creed,
church, or political policy, or guide or occasion for linguistic scholarship and archaeology."

3F.26   KNIGHT, G. WILSON.   The Christian Renaissance.   Revised edition.   London: Methuen, 1962.   368 pp.
        Over half of this study focuses on the Bible as literature.
Special attention is given to the New Testament as an art form,
and to the Gospels and the writings of Paul.   Some coverage of
the Old Testament, passim, and the apocryphal Gospel of Thomas.

3F.27   LEWIS, C. S. <u>Miracles: A Preliminary Study</u>. New York: Macmillan, 1947. 220 pp., passim.
In the course of attacking the traditional academic disbelief in the possibility of miracles, Lewis considers biblical miracles in connection with (among other things) the status of metaphor, symbol, and imaginative response.

3F.28   MACARTHUR, JOHN ROBERTSON. <u>Biblical Literature and Its Backgrounds</u>. New York: Appleton-Century-Crofts, 1936. 547 pp.
An older study providing literary background on the Bible and the individual books of both Testaments and the Apocrypha. Bibliography.

3F.29   MOLLENKOTT, VIRGINIA R. "Speaking for Itself." <u>Christianity Today</u>, 18 (1974), 1355-1357.
Favorable review of 3F.40.

3F.30   MOULTON, RICHARD G. <u>A Short Introduction to the Literature of the Bible</u>. Boston: D. C. Heath, 1909. 382 pp.
An older book designed to aid the general reader in approaching the Bible as literature. Considers biblical history and story, and biblical poetry and prose.

3F.31   PENNIMAN, JOSIAH H. <u>A Book about the English Bible</u>. New York: Macmillan, 1920. 456 pp.
An older study providing background and commentary on parts of the Bible as literature. Includes a survey of the history of the English Bible. Bibliography.

3F.32   PHELPS, WILLIAM LYON. <u>Reading the Bible</u>. New York: Macmillan, 1926. 141 pp.
Three lectures: "Reading the Bible," "St. Paul as a Letter Writer," and "Short Stories in the Bible," by a professor of English literature.

3F.33   REID, MARY ESSON, ed. <u>The Bible Read as Literature: An Anthology</u>. Cleveland: Howard Allen, 1959. 389 pp.
A collection of essays and excerpts providing background and criticism. Includes selections from biblical scholars and from literary critics dating back to the Renaissance. Bibliography. <u>See</u> 1C.30; 3D.7; 3E.7, 10, 15, 21, 23-24; 4C.23; 4E.26; 4F.1; 5C.1.

3F.34   RYKEN, LELAND. <u>The Literature of the Bible</u>. Grand Rapids, Michigan: Zondervan Publishing House, 1974. 364 pp.
A study of selected literary forms in the Bible by an evangelical Christian and professor of English. "I have written

for readers of the Bible who wish to understand and enjoy the
literary dimension of the Bible and who wish to fit biblical
literature into their experience of literature generally."
Illustrations and glossary. See 3D.9; 3F.2, 14.

3F.35   SCHNEIDAU, HERBERT N. "Like Father, Like Son: The Bible,
the Generation Gap, and History." Centennial Review (Michigan
State University), 15 (1971), 296-308.
A study of the modern American "generation gap" which includes some observations on the history of the biblical father
image.

3F.36   SCHNEIDAU, HERBERT N. Sacred Discontent: The Bible and
Western Tradition. Berkeley: University of California Press,
1976. 345 pp.
Studies the Bible in the context of Western culture. The
writers of the Bible reacted against traditions and mythologies in the ancient world and began a tradition of analyzing
and remaking ways of life. Traces this new tradition from the
Bible through Western civilization and literature.
Bibliography.

3F.37   SPRAU, GEORGE. Literature in the Bible. New York: Macmillan, 1932. 454 pp.
Addressed primarily to college students, to help them study
the Bible as they would "any other great book or body of great
literature." Introductory chapters on the Bible, its history,
and the history of Israel are followed by sections on the Law,
the Prophets, the Writings, the Apocrypha, and the New Testament. Bibliography.

3F.38   SYPHERD, WILBUR OWEN. The Literature of the English Bible.
New York: Oxford University Press, 1938. 230 pp.
An early attempt to study the Bible as English literature.
Introductory chapters on the Bible and its development, fol-
lowed by sections on both Testaments and the Apocrypha; mate-
rial in each section organized according to literary type.
Bibliography.

3F.39   VAHANIAN, GABRIEL. "Biblical Symbolism and Man's Religious
Quest." Journal of Religion, 38 (1958), 226-239.
Discusses the nature of symbolism in relation to biblical
myth and language. Biblical symbols are generally rooted in
things of this world.

3F.40   VEDRAL, JOYCE L. A Literary Survey of the Bible. Edited
by Dennis Baker. Plainfield, New Jersey: Logos International,
1973. 265 pp.

A student text containing commentary and study questions on various aspects of the Bible. Bibliography. Teacher's manual available. See 3D.9; 3F.29.

3F.41   WATTS, HAROLD H. The Modern Reader's Guide to the Bible. Revised edition. New York: Harper & Brothers, 1959. 557 pp.
Chapters on the various literary forms in both Testaments and the Apocrypha. "It is one of the intentions of this guide to give an exact, continuous description of the gap that . . . sets the Scriptures apart from other bodies of literature." Bibliography.

3F.42   WHITEHEAD, ALFRED NORTH. Dialogues. Recorded by Lucien Price. Boston: Little, Brown, 1954. 396 pp., passim.
Informal observations on several aspects of the Bible, including its lack of humor, its relation to Greek literature, and its value as a source of allusions and suggestive language.

3F.43   WHITNEY, JOHN R., and SUSAN W. HOWE   Religious Literature of the West. Minneapolis: Augsburg Publishing House, 1971. 315 pp.
A high school text containing background, commentaries, and discussion questions for use by students and teachers. Covers religious literature from both Testaments and the Apocrypha, in addition to the rabbinic writings and the Moslem Qur'an.

3F.44   WILD, LAURA H. A Literary Guide to the Bible: A Study of the Types of Literature Present in the Old and New Testaments. Norwood Editions, 1977. 283 pp.
Reprint of a 1922 work. An older study of genres in the Bible. Focuses on folklore, storytelling, history, poetry, dramatic literature, wisdom literature, oratory, and essay. Chapter bibliographies.

3F.45   WILDER, AMOS. "Theology and Aesthetic Judgment." Chapter 3 in his Theology and Modern Literature. Cambridge, Massachusetts: Harvard University Press, 1958, pp. 63-   .
The first half of this chapter (pp. 63-79) reviews Auerbach's comments on biblical style (see 5C.1 and 8E.1), notes the attitude toward art and classicism reflected in the New Testament (especially Paul), and argues that much modern affection for the King James Bible may be "very much a matter of sheer familiarity."

3F.46   WOOD, IRVING FRANCIS, and ELIHU GRANT. The Bible as Literature: An Introduction. Bible Study Textbook Series. New York: Abingdon Press, 1914. 346 pp.

3G Narrative

An older college text providing background for a literary study of the Bible. Books are treated chronologically according to the date of their composition. Bibliography.

3G The Bible as Literature: Narrative

See also 3A.3; 3F.12, 30, 32; 3L.1; 3M.5; 4F; 7F.

3G.1 ALTER, ROBERT. "Biblical Narrative." Commentary, 61 (May 1976), 61-67.
A literary study of the use of repetition in biblical narrative. See letter of response and rejoinder in Commentary, 62 (October 1976), 24-26.

3G.2 HEIN, ROLLAND N. "A Biblical View of the Novel." Christianity Today, 17 (5 January 1973), 17-19.
While this article presents a fundamentalist biblical justification for reading secular novels, it cites as evidence stories from the Bible that work as literature.

3G.3 KURZWEIL, BARUCH. "Is There Such a Thing as Biblical Tragedy?" Translated by M. Z. Frank. In An Anthology of Hebrew Essays. Edited by Israel Cohen and B. Y. Michali. Tel Aviv: Massada Publishing Company, 1966, volume 1, pp. 97-116.
Argues that biblical narratives can only be seen as tragedies by ignoring their context and forcing on them "the subjective approach of the secular, uncommitted artist."

3G.4 PRICE, REYNOLDS. A Palpable God: Thirty Stories Translated from the Bible with an Essay on the Origins and Life of Narrative. New York: Atheneum, 1978. 205 pp.
The introductory essay, "A Single Meaning: Notes on the Origins and Life of Narrative" (pp. 3-46), and the "Note on Translation and Selection" (pp. 47-60) provide "a prefatory set of questions and considered guesses on the origin, behavior, and destination of story--the chief means by which we became, and stay, human." Biblical narratives are discussed extensively for illustration. The "translations" are retellings of English translations of the stories, occasionally supplemented by references to earlier texts.

3G.5 RAPHAEL, D. D. "Tragedy and Religion." Chapter 2 in The Paradox of Tragedy. Bloomington: Indiana University Press, 1960, pp. 37-51.
A discussion of the incompatibility of tragedy and religion, citing Job as one example. Part reprinted in 5L.36.

3G.6   SCHOLES, ROBERT, and ROBERT KELLOGG. The Nature of Narrative. New York: Oxford University Press, 1966. 326 pp.,
passim.
         A study of the history and nature of narrative. Includes a
brief account of Augustine's reading of Scripture as allegory
(pp. 121-128) and occasional comments on narrative in several
biblical books.

3G.7   SIMON, ULRICH. Story and Faith in the Biblical Narrative.
London: SPCK, 1975. 136 pp.
         A study of the forms of biblical narrative and their coun-
terparts in modern literature. Treats selected narratives
from both Testaments. Argues that "different forms of narrative derived from, and aimed at, different areas of faith."
Bibliography.

3G.8   STERNBERG, MEIR. "Delicate Balance in the Story of the
Rape of Dinah: Biblical Narrative and the Rhetoric of the Narrative Text." Ha-Sifrut, 4 (1973), Hebrew original, pp. 193-
231; English summary, p. xiii.
         Discusses differences between judgments made in everyday
life and those made when reading a literary text and describes
the devices a text may use to channel judgments. Analyzes the
rape of Dinah (Genesis 34) as an example.

3G.9   ZUCK, JOHN E. "Tales of Wonder: Biblical Narrative, Myth,
and Faith Stories." Journal of the American Academy of Religion, 44 (1976), 299-308.
         Compares the work of Hans Frei (3E.4), Mircea Eliade
(3J.4-5), and J. R. R. Tolkien (7H.3) to argue that biblical
narratives and fairy tales have serious common roots in
mythopoesis.

3H   The Bible as Literature: Poetry and Poetics

See also 3A.7; 3E.2, 23-24; 3F.12, 30, 44; 3M.5; 4G; 7G; 8I.2.

3H.1   BAROWAY, ISRAEL. "The Accentual Theory of Hebrew Prosody:
A Further Study in Renaissance Interpretation of Biblical
Form." English Literary History, 17 (1950), 115-135.
         While focusing on Renaissance views of Hebrew prosody, this
study reveals a good deal about the technical aspects of biblical poetry.

3H.2   BROWN, STEPHEN J. Image and Truth: Studies in the Imagery
of the Bible. Rome: Catholic Book Agency, 1955. 161 pp.

3H Poetry and Poetics

Studies the nature of imagery, metaphor, and symbolism in both Testaments.

3H.3 FREEDMAN, DAVID NOEL. "Pottery, Poetry, and Prophecy: An Essay on Biblical Poetry." Journal of Biblical Literature, 96 (1977), 5-26.
A scholarly discussion of the character and function of biblical poetry.

3H.4 HATTO, ARTHUR T., ed. EOS: An Enquiry into the Theme of Lovers' Meetings and Partings at Dawn in Poetry. The Hague: Mouton & Company, 1965. 854 pp., passim.
A "collection of poetry from all over the world about lovers at dawn, together with what commentary we can offer. . . ." Includes a discussion of dawn imagery throughout the Bible and an analysis of the Song of Songs as part of this tradition (pp. 203-209). Illustrations.

3I The Bible as Literature: Allegory

See also 3D.8; 3E.9, 14; 3G.6; 8C.3.

3I.1 FLETCHER, ANGUS. Allegory: The Theory of a Symbolic Mode. Ithaca, New York: Cornell University Press, 1964. 432 pp.
A survey of allegory, its components, and its types. Provides literary background for a traditional way of reading much of the Bible. Bibliography.

3I.2 MACQUEEN, JOHN. "Biblical Allegory." Chapter 2 in his Allegory. The Critical Idiom, No. 14. London: Methuen, 1970, pp. 18-36.
Discusses several kinds of biblical allegory with particular attention to typology, Jesus' parables, and Revelation. Bibliography.

3J The Bible as Literature: Myth and Legend

See also 3C.3; 3F.6, 36, 39; 3G.9; 3K.5; 4I; 7H.

3J.1 BODKIN, MAUD. Studies of Type Images in Poetry, Religion, and Philosophy. London: Oxford University Press, 1951. 196 pp.
A series of essays tracing three archetypal images--of God, of the Divine Birth, and of Wisdom--in various writings including the Bible.

3J.2   CAMPBELL, JOSEPH. The Hero with a Thousand Faces. Bollin-
         gen Series, No. 17. Second edition. Princeton: Princeton
         University Press, 1968. 440 pp.
              A psychoanalytic approach to mythology. Discusses myths
         and folktales from all over the world including some from the
         Bible.

3J.3   CAMPBELL, JOSEPH, ed. Myths, Dreams, and Religion. New
         York: E. P. Dutton, 1970. 255 pp., passim.
              An anthology of essays on myth by various scholars designed
         for lay readers. Includes John F. Priest, "Myth and Dream in
         Hebrew Scripture" (pp. 48-67), and Amos N. Wilder, "Myth and
         Dream in Christian Scripture" (pp. 68-90; reprinted with re-
         visions as "The Symbolics of the New Testament" in Wilder's
         The New Voice. New York: Herder and Herder, 1969, pp. 99-122).

3J.4   ELIADE, MIRCEA. Cosmos and History: The Myth of the Eter-
         nal Return. Translated by Willard R. Trask. New York: Harper
         & Brothers, 1969. 192 pp., passim.
              A study of the tendency of earlier civilizations to view
         time as a series of recurring patterns. Background on a mythi-
         cal view of the world with scattered references to biblical
         passages. See 3G.9.

3J.5   ELIADE, MIRCEA. The Sacred and the Profane: The Nature of
         Religion. Translated by Willard R. Trask. New York: Harcourt,
         Brace & World, 1959. 256 pp.
              A study of mythic-archetypal patterns involving space,
         time, nature, and life. Bibliography. See 3G.9.

3J.6   FRAZER, JAMES GEORGE. The New Golden Bough. Edited by
         Theodor H. Gaster. New York: S. G. Phillips, 1959. 768 pp.
              A condensation and updating of Frazer's classic twelve-
         volume study. Describes primitive myths on several themes,
         providing mythological contexts and parallels for many bibli-
         cal stories.

3J.7   FRYE, NORTHROP. Anatomy of Criticism: Four Essays. Prince-
         ton: Princeton University Press, 1971. 393 pp.
              A major attempt to define the general framework of literary
         criticism. Does not discuss specific biblical texts in depth,
         but provides important insights on myth and archetypal criti-
         cism as well as other critical modes. Includes a call for a
         study of the Bible as literature (see, e.g., p. 315).

3J.8   FRYE, NORTHROP. The Educated Imagination. Bloomington:
         Indiana University Press, 1964. 159 pp.

3J   Myth and Legend

These six lectures (originally radio talks) refer directly to the Bible only here and there, but they present a theory of the relationship between literature and mythology that elucidates the concept of the Bible as literature. Frye argues that the myth of the Bible should be the basis of all literary training.

3J.9   FRYE, NORTHROP. "History and Myth in the Bible," in The Literature of Fact: Selected Papers from the English Institute. Edited by Angus Fletcher. New York: Columbia University Press, 1976, pp. 1-19.
A defense of the Bible as a literary work which "demands a literary response from us." The Bible is a prerequisite to the study of literature because it has provided a "mythological framework" for Western literature.

3J.10   FRYE, NORTHROP. The Secular Scripture: A Study in the Structure of Romance. Cambridge, Massachusetts: Harvard University Press, 1976. 209 pp.
Lectures on the genre of romance, providing background on myth. Built around Frye's contention that the Bible has provided a mythological framework for Western literature. Cites the Bible, passim, for reference and illustration.

3J.11   HOOKE, S. H. Middle Eastern Mythology. Baltimore: Penguin Books, 1963. 199 pp.
An introductory study of the mythology of Israel and her Middle Eastern neighbors. Includes chapters on the mythology of the Old and New Testaments and the Apocrypha. Bibliography.

3J.12   JUNG, C. G., and C. KERÉNYI. Introduction to a Science of Mythology: The Myth of the Divine Child and the Mysteries of Eleusis. Translated by R. F. C. Hull. London: Routledge & Kegan Paul, 1951. 289 pp.
Essays focusing on the connection between mythology and origins. Background for myth in the Bible.

3J.13   KRAMER, SAMUEL NOAH. Mythologies of the Ancient World. An Anchor Book. Garden City, New York: Doubleday, 1961. 480 pp.
Essays by various scholars discussing the mythologies of different sections of the ancient world. Particularly relevant to a literary understanding of the Bible are the essays on Egypt, Sumer and Akkad, and Canaan.

3J.14   LANGER, SUSANNE K. Philosophy in a New Key: A Study in the Symbolism of Reason, Rite, and Art. Third edition. Cambridge, Massachusetts: Harvard University Press, 1960. 333 pp., passim.

While it does not treat the Bible directly, this study of symbolism provides background on myth and art.

3J.15   LEACH, EDMUND. Genesis as Myth and Other Essays. London: Jonathan Cape, 1969. 124 pp.
In the title essay (pp. 7-23), a social anthropologist analyzes Genesis as myth, defining the latter as "observable phenomena which are the expression of unobservable realities." The other essays in this volume: "The Legitimacy of Solomon" (pp. 25-83), and "Virgin Birth" (pp. 85-112), offer similar approaches to these biblical subjects. The essay on Solomon is reprinted in Introduction to Structuralism. Edited by Michael Lane. New York: Basic Books, 1970, pp. 268-277.

3J.16   LEEMING, DAVID ADAMS. Mythology: The Voyage of the Hero. Philadelphia: J. B. Lippincott, 1973. 348 pp.
Excerpts from the stories of selected heroes (including Moses and Jesus) illustrate eight stages in the life of the mythical hero, from miraculous conception and birth to ascension and apotheosis. Provides a mythological context for these two major biblical heroes. Bibliography.

3J.17   NEUMANN, ERICH. The Origins and History of Consciousness. Bollingen Series, No. 42. Translated by R. F. C. Hull. Third printing, with revision. Princeton: Princeton University Press, 1970. 520 pp., passim.
A study of depth psychology providing background on a Jungian approach to the mythological stages in the evolution of consciousness. Treats the myths of creation, of the hero, and of transformation, and includes references to their appearance in the Bible. Bibliography.

3J.18   NIEBUHR, REINHOLD. Beyond Tragedy: Essays on the Christian Interpretation of History. New York: Charles Scribner's Sons, 1937. 318 pp., passim.
Fifteen essays offer observations about "the valid contribution of myth to the biblical world view" and the relationship between tragedy and a Christian view of history.

3J.19   RAGLAN, FITZROY. The Hero: A Study in Tradition, Myth, and Drama. New York: Vintage Books, 1956. 317 pp., passim.
Argues that most ancient traditions have no historical basis but are mythological. Background on ancient myth and hero worshop, with occasional illustrations from the Bible. Bibliography.

The Bible as a Whole

3K Language and Linguistics

3K The Bible as Literature: Language and Linguistics

See also 1C.8; 1D.8; 3C.3; 3D.2; 3F.23, 39; 3L; 4J; 7I.J.

3K.1   ALONSO SCHÖKEL, LUIS. The Inspired Word: Scripture in the Light of Language and Literature. Translated by Francis Martin. New York: Herder and Herder, 1965. 418 pp.
Addressed to "the educated Christian public" by a Jesuit author. Brings to a study of the Bible "the categories and acquisitions of the philosophy of language and literary analysis." Chapters on the word divine and human, the inspired word, the inspired authors, the inspired work, and the consequences of inspiration.

3K.2   BARR, JAMES. The Semantics of Biblical Language. London: Oxford University Press, 1961. 323 pp.
An advanced text presupposing some knowledge of the biblical languages. "A survey of the way in which the meaning of biblical language is understood, . . . and the criticism of certain methods . . . of using linguistic evidence from the Bible."

3K.3   HOPPER, STANLEY ROMAINE, and DAVID L. MILLER, eds. Interpretation: The Poetry of Meaning. New York: Harcourt, Brace & World, 1967. 159 pp.
Major addresses from a symposium on "Metaphor, Symbol, Image, and Meaning" held at Drew University in 1966. Background on the new roles of language and poetics in religious experience. Contents: Norman O. Brown, "Apocalypse: The Place of Mystery in the Life of the Mind" (pp. 7-13); Heinrich Ott, "Hermeneutics and Personhood" (pp. 14-34); Julian Marias, "Philosophic Truth and the Metaphoric System" (pp. 40-53); Owen Barfield, "Imagination and Inspiration" (pp. 54-76); Kenneth Burke, A Theory of Terminology" (pp. 83-102); Beda Allemann, "Metaphor and Antimetaphor" (pp. 103-123). Bibliography.

3K.4   LAPOINTE, ROGER. "The New Status of Language." Catholic Biblical Quarterly, 36 (1974), 233-236.
Studies the relation between language and theology. "Language has replaced reason as the ultimate foundation of knowledge." Background for structuralist and linguistic analyses of the Bible.

3K.5   THOMPSON, LEONARD L. Introducing Biblical Literature: A More Fantastic Country. Englewood Cliffs, New Jersey: Prentice-Hall, 1978. 366 pp.
A study of the language of the Bible and of the "fantastic world" biblical words create. Covers both Testaments and

considers such things as syntax, irony, myth, image, and metaphor. Illustrations and bibliography.

3K.6   WHEELWRIGHT, PHILIP. The Burning Fountain: A Study in the
Language of Symbolism. New and revised edition. Bloomington:
Indiana University Press, 1968. 316 pp., passim.
A study of the nature and types of symbolic language. Pro-
vides background on the nature of literary expression, occa-
sionally citing the Bible for illustration.

3L   The Bible as Literature: Structuralism

See also 2E.2; 3J.15; 3K; 4K; 7J.

3L.1   CROSSAN, JOHN DOMINIC, ed. "Paul Ricoeur on Biblical Hermeneutics." Semeia, 4 (1975). 154 pp.
Three articles on biblical hermeneutics by a specialist in
the philosophy of language: "The Narrative Form," "The Meta-
phorical Process," and "The Specificity of Religious Language."
Also contains an introduction and bibliography on Ricoeur's
work in biblical interpretation by Loretta Dornisch.

3L.2   DOTY, WILLIAM G. "Fundamental Questions about Literary-
Critical Methodology: A Review Article." Journal of the American Academy of Religion, 40 (1972), 521-527.
An essay review of Erhardt Güttgemans' *Offene Fragen zur
Formgeschichte des Evangeliums (1971). Güttgemans emphasizes
the limitations of modern biblical criticism and sees the need
to adopt the methods of current linguistic and secular literary
analysis. Background for a structuralist approach to the
Bible. See 3L.3 and 3L.7.

3L.3   DOTY, WILLIAM G. "Linguistics and Biblical Criticism."
Journal of the American Academy of Religion, 41 (1973), 114-
121.
An essay review of the generative poetics research team at
Bonn led by Erhardt Güttgemans. Background for structuralism
and linguistic approaches to the Bible. Argues "the necessity
to conjoin the best insights of new and old toward the final
task of . . . 'moving across' . . . the now almost infinite
chasm between the contexts of late antiquity and the present."
See 3L.2 and 3L.7.

3L.4   Interpretation: A Journal of Bible and Theology. Volume 28,
no. 2 (April 1974).
Articles on biblical structuralism for beginners. Contains
three general studies: Robert A. Spivey, "Structuralism and

3L Structuralism

Biblical Studies: The Uninvited Guest," pp. 133-145; Richard
Jacobson, "The Structuralists and the Bible," pp. 146-164; and
Robert C. Culley, "Structural Analysis: Is It Done with Mir-
rors?" pp. 165-181, and two applications of structuralism to
specific sections of the Bible: Job (5L.30) and Paul (8L.19).
Each article has helpful bibliographical references.

3L.5   JOHNSON, ALFRED M., JR., ed. Structural Analysis and Biblical Exegesis: Interpretational Essays by R. Barthes, F.
Bovon, F.-J. Leenhardt, R. Martin-Achard, and J. Starobinski.
Pittsburgh Theological Monograph Series, No. 3. Pittsburgh:
Pickwick Press, 1974. 173 pp.
    A translation of a French collection. A general essay on
the subject is followed by two studies each of Genesis 32:23-
33 and Mark 5:1-20. Bibliography.

3L.6   PATTE, DANIEL. What Is Structural Exegesis? Guides to Biblical Scholarship, New Testament Series. Philadelphia: Fortress Press, 1976. 96 pp.
    A brief introduction to structuralism and its relationship
to biblical studies. Annotated bibliography.

3L.7   PETERSEN, NORMAN R., ed. "Erhardt Güttgemans' 'Generative
Poetics.'" Translated by William G. Doty. Semeia, 6 (1976).
236 pp.
    Four essays by Güttgemanns defining generative poetics as
an exegetical method and applying it to a structural study of
the New Testament. See 3L.2-3.

3L.8   POLZIN, ROBERT M. Biblical Structuralism: Method and Sub-
jectivity in the Study of Ancient Texts. Semeia Supplements.
Philadelphia: Fortress Press, 1977. 224 pp.
    A general description of structuralism, followed by a struc-
tural analysis of Job and an analysis of three classics of
biblical criticism (studies by Wellhausen, von Rad, and Noth)
as structural analyses. Bibliography.

3L.9   SCHOLES, ROBERT. Structuralism in Literature: An Introduction. New Haven: Yale University Press, 1974. 233 pp.
    Though it does not treat the Bible specifically, this sur-
vey is an important introduction to the nature, history, and
uses of structuralism in literature for the beginner.
Bibliography.

3L.10   WITTIG, SUSAN, ed. Structuralism: An Interdisciplinary
Study. Pittsburgh Reprint Series, No. 3. Pittsburgh: Pickwick Press, 1975. 162 pp.

Reprint of the Summer 1975 issue of the journal Soundings (volume 58, no. 2). General essays on structuralism; the following relate to the Bible as literature: Joseph Blenkinsopp, "The Search for the Prickly Plant: Structure and Function in the Gilgamesh Epic" (see 4D.2; 5C.4; and 8C.15).

3M The Bible as Literature: Pedagogical Concerns

See also 1B; 3D.3, 9-10; 3F.40, 43; 4E.1; 7E.6; 8B.3.

3M.1   "The Bible as Culture." Time, 94 (3 October 1969), 80-82.
Discusses attempts to treat the Bible in public schools in the light of Supreme Court decisions. Reviews 1B.1 as one attempt to deal with the problem.

3M.2   CAPPS, ALTON C. "A Realistic Approach to Biblical Literature." English Journal, 58 (1969), 230-235.
Argues that biblical literature should be taught in public schools for cultural, if not religious, reasons. Includes suggested course outline.

3M.3   DIETERICH, DAVID J., and JANE MCCLELLAN. "ERIC/RCS Review: Teaching the Bible as Literature." Indiana English Journal, 10, no. 3 (Spring 1976), 35-37.
A brief note reviewing the legal implications of teaching the Bible in public schools and surveying some of the curriculum materials and source books available for teachers. Aimed primarily at secondary school teachers. Bibliography.

3M.4   HOGAN, ROBERT F. "The Bible in the English Program." English Journal, 54 (1965), 488-494.
A study of the state of Bible as literature courses in American secondary schools before and after the Supreme Court decision (1963) outlawing devotional reading of the Bible in public schools.

3M.5   LANTZ, J[OHN] EDWARD. Reading the Bible Aloud. New York: Macmillan, 1959. 158 pp.
Information on public reading of the Bible. Aimed primarily at ministers, but covers techniques of oral interpretation of the literature of the Bible. Potentially useful for classroom work. Appendixes include lists of narrative and poetry in the Bible. Bibliography.

3M.6   MCCULLEY, CECIL M. "Teaching the Bible as Literature." Christian Century, 78 (1961), 357-358.

3M   Pedagogical Concerns

> Justifies studying the Bible as literature in the light of students' rights and ultimate spiritual benefits.

3M. 7   MEADOR, MELBA. "Bringing Job into the Twentieth Century." *English Journal*, 60 (1971), 921-923.
Suggestions on teaching Job in contemporary high school English classes.

3M. 8   NEUMEYER, PETER F. "What Is Relevant Literature?" *Teachers College Record*, 71 (1969), 1-9.
Argues that great literature is always relevant, even to the nontraditional student, because it deals with basic human problems. Comments on the stories of Job, Abraham and Isaac, and Noah for illustration.

3M. 9   PHELPS, WILLIAM LYON. "Reading the Bible." *Proceedings and Papers of the Indiana State Teachers' Association* (1917), 140-147.
An older plea for treating the Bible as a literary monument in our schools.

3M. 10   SPITZER, GARY. "Teaching the Bible as Literature: Problems and Possibilities." *Journal of General Education*, 21 (1969), 183-191.
Discusses how a teacher of literature should handle the history, theology, didacticism, and inconsistencies which are part of the Bible.

3M. 11   WADDY, LAWRENCE. *The Bible as Drama*. New York: Paulist Press, 1975. 292 pp.
Ninety Bible stories presented as plays. A "do-it-yourself" book appropriate for use in a secondary or collegiate classroom as an aid to getting students "involved" by having them act out the stories.

3M. 12   WALTON, ROBERT C. *A Source Book of the Bible for Teachers*. London: SCM Press, 1970. 415 pp.
An anthology of commentaries by various noted scholars designed for teachers in British schools. Contains introductory information on many aspects of all parts of the Bible. Maps.

3M. 13   WARSHAW, THAYER S. *Handbook for Teaching the Bible in Literature Courses*. Nashville: Abingdon Press, 1978. 416 pp.
A guide for teachers at the secondary or collegiate levels. Surveys ways of approaching the Bible and problems arising from the different religious sensibilities of students. Includes teaching aids, practical suggestions, and study questions. A glossary defines biblical, scholarly, and religious terms a teacher may encounter in background reading.

The Bible as a Whole

3M.14   WARSHAW, THAYER S. "Studying the Bible in Public School."
English Journal, 53 (1964), 91-100.
   An argument for teaching the Bible as part of the humanities
in public schools and a description of one teacher's approaches
to it.

3M.15   WARSHAW, THAYER S. "Teaching English Teachers to Teach
the Bible: The Indiana University Model." Indiana Social
Studies Quarterly, 25, no. 1 (Spring 1972), 110-118.
   A discussion of some of the problems inherent in approaching
the Bible as literature in the classroom and of the attempts
to deal with them at the annual Indiana University Institute
on Teaching the Bible as Literature.

3M.16   WARSHAW, THAYER S. "Teaching the Bible as Literature."
English Journal, 58 (1969), 571-576.
   A discussion of some of the alternatives available for use
of the Bible in the English classroom.

3M.17   WARSHAW, THAYER S., BETTY LOU MILLER, with JAMES S.
ACKERMAN. Bible-Related Curriculum Materials: A Bibliography.
Nashville: Abingdon Press, 1976. 178 pp.
   An extensive list of items suggested mostly by secondary
school teachers. "There is no attempt to be definitive or
complete." Treats the Bible and literature, in literature,
and as literature. Chapters on biblical stories: Creation,
Garden of Eden, Cain and Abel, etc.

4   The Old Testament as a Whole

4A   The Old Testament: Historical and Cultural Background

See also 2C; 2D; 2E.12; 2I.3; 3B; 4B.1; 4C.23; 4E; 5A.9; 5C.3; 5D.9; 5H.5, 9.

4A.1   ANDERSON, G. W.   The History and Religion of Israel.   New York: Oxford University Press, 1966.   222 pp.
Surveys the history and religion of the Hebrews chronologically through the Maccabean Revolt.   Illustrations.

4A.2   BICKERMAN, ELIAS.   From Ezra to the Last of the Maccabees: Foundations of Post-Biblical Judaism.   New York: Schocken Books, 1962.   186 pp.
Provides historical background for later Old Testament and Apocryphal writings.

4A.3   BRIGHT, JOHN.   A History of Israel.   Second edition.   The Old Testament Library.   London: SCM Press, 1972.   536 pp.
Begins with the prehistory of Israel's ancestors and runs through the end of the Old Testament period.   Bibliography and maps.

4A.4   FRANKFORT, HENRI.   The Birth of Civilization in the Near East.   Garden City, New York: Doubleday, 1956.   158 pp.
A study of the social and political history of ancient Egypt and Mesopotamia.

4A.5   GOODSPEED, EDGAR J.   The Story of the Bible.   Chicago: University of Chicago Press, 1957.   176 pp.
Short commentaries on the historical situation out of which each book of the Old Testament grew.   Books are arranged in order of composition.

4A.6   GURNEY, O. R.   The Hittites.   Revised edition.   Baltimore: Penguin Books, 1961.   256 pp.
The history and culture of a nation that interacts with Israel in the Old Testament.   Includes a chapter on Hittite literature.   Bibliography.

The Old Testament as a Whole

4A Historical & Cultural Background

4A.7   HEATON, E. W. <u>Everyday Life in Old Testament Times</u>. New
York: Charles Scribner's Sons, 1956. 240 pp.
Presents "a panorama of Israelite life, as ordinary families
knew it, from about 1250 to 586 B.C." <u>See</u> 7A.1.

4A.8   HUNT, IGNATIUS. <u>The World of the Patriarchs</u>. Backgrounds
to the Bible Series. Englewood Cliffs, New Jersey: Prentice-
Hall, 1967. 192 pp.
Historical and cultural background on the patriarchs from
the beginnings of the Hebrew race to Joseph. Chapter
bibliographies.

4A.9   JAMES, E. O. <u>The Ancient Gods: The History and Diffusion
of Religion in the Ancient Near East and the Eastern Mediter-
ranean</u>. Putnam History of Religion. New York: G. P. Putnam's
Sons, 1960. 359 pp.
Background on the religion of ancient Israel. Bibliography.

4A.10   KAUFMANN, YEHEZKEL. <u>The Religion of Israel: From Its Beginnings to the Babylonian Exile</u>. Translated by Moshe Greenberg.
Chicago: University of Chicago Press, 1960. 498 pp.
An abridgement of the first seven volumes of an eight-volume
Hebrew work. Studies the nature and history of Israelite religion, arguing that it was "an original creation of the people
of Israel." Sees the Torah as "the literary product of the
earliest stage of Israelite religion, . . . prior to literary
prophecy."

4A.11   MCKENZIE, JOHN L. <u>The World of the Judges</u>. Backgrounds to
the Bible Series. Englewood Cliffs, New Jersey: Prentice-Hall,
1966. 192 pp.
Historical and cultural background on the period from Israel's entrance into Canaan until the monarchy (the books of
Joshua and Judges). Chapter bibliographies.

4A.12   MALY, EUGENE H. <u>The World of David and Solomon</u>. Backgrounds to the Bible Series. Englewood Cliffs, New Jersey:
Prentice-Hall, 1966. 192 pp.
Historical and cultural background on the Israelite monarchy from Saul to Solomon. Chapter bibliographies.

4A.13   MEEK, THEOPILE JAMES. <u>Hebrew Origins</u>. Revised edition.
New York: Harper & Brothers, 1960. 256 pp.
Traces the origins of the Hebrews and their concepts of law,
God, the priesthood, prophecy, and monotheism.

4A.14   MOSCATI, SABATINO. <u>The Face of the Ancient Orient</u>. London:
Routledge & Kegan Paul, 1960. 342 pp.

Compares the cultures of several ancient Near Eastern civilizations. Comments on their history, religious structure, literary genres, and artistic types. Includes excerpts from these ancient literatures. Illustrations.

4A.15   MUILENBURG, JAMES. The Way of Israel: Biblical Faith and Ethics. Religious Perspectives, Vol. 5. New York: Harper & Brothers, 1961. 158 pp.
An examination of the ethics and ethos of ancient Israel through a study of biblical narrative, poetry, and other forms of utterance. Bibliography.

4A.16   MYERS, J. M. The World of the Restoration. Backgrounds to the Bible Series. Englewood Cliffs, New Jersey: Prentice-Hall, 1968. 192 pp.
Historical and cultural background of Israel from the end of the Babylonian captivity to the last half of the fourth century B.C. Bibliography.

4A.17   ORLINSKY, HARRY M. Ancient Israel. The Development of Western Civilization. Ithaca, New York: Cornell University Press, 1954. 207 pp.
A history of Israel through Old Testament times. Bibliography.

4A.18   PEDERSEN, JOHANNES. Israel: Its Life and Culture. Four volumes, bound in two. London: Oxford University Press, 1926-1940.
A thorough study of the culture of ancient Israel.

4A.19   PRITCHARD, JAMES B. The Ancient Near East in Pictures Relating to the Old Testament. Second edition with supplement. Princeton: Princeton University Press, 1969. 414 pp.
Over eight hundred photographs of monuments and artifacts illustrating Old Testament history. A catalogue offers explanations of the pictures. Maps. See 4D.10, 11.

4A.20   ROBINSON, H. WHEELER. Corporate Personality in Ancient Israel. Facet Books Biblical Series, No. 11. Philadelphia: Fortress Press, 1964. 56 pp.
Background on the relationship between the individual and the group in ancient Israelite thought. Particular reference to the "I" in the Psalms and the Servant Songs in Second Isaiah. Bibliography.

4A.21   SMEND, RUDOLF. Yahweh War and Tribal Confederation: Reflections upon Israel's Earliest History. Translated by Max Gray Rogers. Nashville: Abingdon Press, 1970. 144 pp.

The Old Testament as a Whole

4A Historical & Cultural Background

        Historical background on the confederation of the Israelite tribes during the Exodus.

4A.22   SMITH, GEORGE ADAM. "The Hebrew Genius as Exhibited in the Old Testament," in The Legacy of Israel. Edited by Edwyn R. Bevan and Charles Singer. Oxford: Clarendon Press, 1965, pp. 1-28.
        Background on the literary, religious, and general aspects of Israelite culture as reflected in the Old Testament.

4A.23   VAUX, ROLAND DE. Ancient Israel: Its Life and Institutions. Translated by John McHugh. Second edition. London: Darton, Longman, & Todd, 1965. 616 pp.
        Background on the culture and society of Israel in Old Testament times. Covers nomadism, and family, civil, military, and religious institutions. Bibliography.

4A.24   WILSON, JOHN A. The Culture of Ancient Egypt. Chicago: University of Chicago Press, 1971. 334 pp.
        Originally published as The Burden of Egypt (1951). Background on the culture of ancient Israel's neighbor and "first enslaver."

4B The Old Testament: Scholarly and Theological Background

See also 1D.36; 2C; 2E.13; 2I.4; 3A.1-2, 6, 13; 3C; 4C; 5C.3, 5; 5H.6; 5Q.12; 6D.3.

4B.1   BUBER, MARTIN. The Prophetic Faith. New York: Harper & Brothers, 1960. 247 pp.
        Traces biblical teaching about the relation between God and Israel from the eighth century to the sixth century B.C. Particular attention to the Song of Deborah (pp. 8-13) and Job (pp. 188-197), among other literary pieces.

4B.2   EICHRODT, WALTHER. Theology of the Old Testament. Two volumes. Translated by J. A. Baker. The Old Testament Library. Philadelphia: Westminster Press, 1961. Volume 1, 542 pp.; volume 2, 573 pp.
        An advanced study providing theological background for the Old Testament.

4B.3   FROMM, ERICH. You Shall Be as Gods: A Radical Interpretation of the Old Testament and Its Tradition. New York: Holt, Rinehart & Winston, 1966. 240 pp.
        A radical humanist interpretation that sees the Old Testament as a revolutionary book depicting the liberation of man. Chapters on Old Testament concepts of God, man, history, sin

and repentance, Halakhah ("the way"), and a special chapter
on the Psalms.

4B.4   MCCARTHY, DENNIS J. Old Testament Covenant: A Survey of
Current Opinions. Growing Points in Theology. Richmond, Vir-
ginia: John Knox Press, 1972. 120 pp.
        Background on the covenant motif in the Old Testament.
Bibliography.

4B.5   RAD, GERHARD VON. Old Testament Theology. Two volumes.
Translated by D. M. G. Stalker. New York: Harper & Row, 1962-
1965. Volume 1, 495 pp.; volume 2, 485 pp.
        An advanced text providing theological background.

4B.6   ROBINSON, H. WHEELER. The Cross in the Old Testament.
Philadelphia: Westminster Press, 1955. 192 pp.
        Three monographs on suffering in Job, Second Isaiah, and
Jeremiah.

4B.7   ROWLEY, H[AROLD] H. The Faith of Israel: Aspects of Old
Testament Thought. Philadelphia: Westminster Press, 1956.
220 pp.
        Background on selected aspects of Old Testament theology.

4B.8   ROWLEY, H[AROLD] H., ed. The Old Testament and Modern
Study: A Generation of Discovery and Research. Oxford:
Clarendon Press, 1952. 437 pp.
        Essays by various scholars providing scholarly and theolo-
gical background on several aspects of Old Testament study.

4B.9   ROWLEY, H[AROLD] H. The Servant of the Lord: And Other
Essays on the Old Testament. Second edition, revised. Oxford:
Basil Blackwell, 1965. 371 pp.
        An anthology of essays providing scholarly background on
aspects of Old Testament study. Of particular interest for
the Bible as literature are "The Marriage of Ruth" (pp. 169-
194; See 5H.9), "The Interpretation of the Song of Songs"
(pp. 195-246), and "The Unity of the Book of Daniel" (pp. 247-
280).

4B.10   SCOTT, R. B. Y. The Way of Wisdom in the Old Testament.
New York: Macmillan, 1971. 256 pp.
        A study of the role of Wisdom in the Old Testament, with
particular attention to Proverbs, Job, and Ecclesiastes, among
others. Companion to 5Q.11.

4B.11   SKEHAN, PATRICK W. Studies in Israelite Poetry and Wisdom.
Catholic Biblical Quarterly, Monograph Series No. 1.

4B Scholarly & Theological Background

Washington, D.C.: Catholic Biblical Association of America,
1971. 277 pp.
   Scholarly background on selected problems in Proverbs,
Psalms, the Song of Moses (Deuteronomy 32:1-43), Job, Ecclesi-
asticus, and Wisdom. Bibliography.

4B.12   WALDOW, HANS EBERHARD VON. "Israel and Her Land: Some
Theological Considerations," in A Light unto My Path: Old
Testament Studies in Honor of Jacob M. Myers. Edited by
Howard N. Bream, Ralph D. Heim, and Carey A. Moore. Philadel-
phia: Temple University Press, 1974, pp. 493-508.
   Provides background on the possibility that this theme may
be "the main idea of an Old Testament theology."

4B.13   WRIGHT, G[EORGE] ERNEST. The Old Testament against Its En-
vironment. Studies in Biblical Theology. London: SCM Press,
1962. 116 pp.
   Theological background on the nature of God, the meaning of
life and history, and the worship and service of God in the
Old Testament. Argues that these elements in Israelite religion are unique and cannot be explained as outgrowths of surrounding cultures.

4C   The Old Testament: Introductions and Commentaries

See also 2H; 4E.

4C.1   ANDERSON, BERNHARD W. Understanding the Old Testament.
Third edition. Englewood Cliffs, New Jersey: Prentice-Hall,
1975. 670 pp.
   Studies the Old Testament in the context of Israelite history. Companion to 7C.10. Illustrations and selected
bibliography.

4C.2   ANDERSON, GEORGE W. A Critical Introduction to the Old
Testament. Studies in Theology. London: Gerald Duckworth,
1974. 270 pp.
   A brief introduction to the Old Testament itself and to the
major recent theories about its nature and composition. Includes a chapter on "Literary Forms and Literary History."
Companion to 7C.4.

4C.3   ARCHER, GLEASON, L., JR. A Survey of Old Testament Introduction. Chicago: Moody Press, 1964. 507 pp.
   A text for beginning college students, containing a series
of general essays on the Old Testament followed by special
introductions to the individual books. Follows "a consistently
conservative or evangelical viewpoint."

4C.4   BEEBE, H. KEITH. The Old Testament. Belmont, California:
Dickenson Publishing Company, 1970. 522 pp.
     A study of the literary sources and historical and religi-
ous traditions behind the Old Testament. Bibliography.

4C.5   BUCK, HARRY M. People of the Lord: The History, Scriptures, and Faith of Ancient Israel. New York: Macmillan,
1966. 671 pp.
     Extensive Old Testament background, chronologically ar-
ranged. Appendix on "The Text of the Bible and Its English
Translations." Bibliographical essay.

4C.6   CORNFELD, GAALYAHU, ed. Adam to Daniel: An Illustrated
Guide to the Old Testament and Its Background. New York:
Macmillan, 1961. 567 pp.
     Background for the general reader prepared by Israeli
scholars. "This new approach to Old Testament literature
sets it against its background as understood in Israel."
Covers each of the major segments of the Old Testament. A
companion, 7C.2, covers the Apocrypha and New Testament.

4C.7   DAICHES, DAVID. "Presenting the Bible," in his More
Literary Essays. Edinburgh: Oliver & Boyd, 1968, pp. 248-267.
     First published in Commentary (September 1965). A review
of the earlier volumes of the Anchor Bible (See 1A.1)--"Genesis," 5A.7; "1 and 2 Chronicles," 5J.1; "Jeremiah," 5S.2;
"Job," 5L.32; "Proverbs and Ecclesiastes," 5N.2--providing
extensive historical, literary, and linguistic background
about these books.

4C.8   EISSFELDT, OTTO. The Old Testament: An Introduction.
Translated by Peter R. Ackroyd. New York: Harper & Row,
1965. 885 pp.
     Covers the formation of Old Testament books from earliest
prose types and sayings to written documents. Includes Apocrypha and Pseudepigrapha, and some Dead Sea Scroll material.

4C.9   GERSH, HARRY. The Sacred Books of the Jews. New York:
Stein & Day, 1968. 256 pp.
     The Old Testament discussed in the context of the Talmud
and other sacred Jewish writings.

4C.10   GOTTWALD, NORMAN K. A Light to the Nations: An Introduction to the Old Testament. New York: Harper & Row, 1959.
638 pp.
     "Throughout there has been an attempt to integrate the
literature, history, and religion, and to point up connec-
tions between the faith of Israel and that of the later syna-
gogue and church." Material arranged roughly chronologically.

The Old Testament as a Whole

4C   Introductions and Commentaries

Recommended further reading. Appendix includes Near Eastern
texts related to the Old Testament.

4C.11   HARRELSON, WALTER. Interpreting the Old Testament. New
York: Holt, Rinehart & Winston, 1964. 543 pp.
A commentary on the literature of the Hebrew Bible.
Bibliography.

4C.12   HERTZ, J. ed. The Pentateuch and Haftorahs: Hebrew Text,
English Translation, and Commentary. Second edition. London:
Soncino Press, 1961. 1067 pp.
A one-volume Jewish commentary.

4C.13   JOHNSON, AUBREY. "The Writings," in 3B.3, pp. 47-51.
A brief introduction to the most literary section of the
Hebrew Bible.

4C.14   KAISER, OTTO. Introduction to the Old Testament: A Presen-
tation of Its Results and Problems. Translated by John Sturdy.
Minneapolis: Augsburg Publishing House, 1975. 438 pp.
Focuses on the historical narratives, the prophetic tradition, and Israelite poetry and wisdom. Bibliography.

4C.15   KUNTZ, J. KENNETH. The People of Ancient Israel: An Introduction to Old Testament Literature, History, and Thought.
New York: Harper & Row, 1974. 575 pp.
An introduction for the nonspecialist, emphasizing the historical approach. Illustrations and maps.

4C.16   MCKENZIE, JOHN L. The Two-Edged Sword: An Interpretation
of the Old Testament. Milwaukee: Bruce Publishing Company,
1956. 335 pp.
A reading of the Old Testament in the Roman Catholic tradition. Bibliography.

4C.17   MORIARTY, FREDERICK L. Introducing the Old Testament. Lon-
don: Burns & Oates, 1960. 267 pp.
This Roman Catholic introduction concentrates on fifteen
Old Testament figures from Abraham to Daniel. Bibliography.

4C.18   NAPIER, B. DAVIE. Song of the Vineyard: A Theological Introduction to the Old Testament. New York: Harper & Row,
1962. 399 pp.
An introduction emphasizing "the meaning of the ancient
text in the life and faith of that ancient people, Israel."
Bibliography.

The Old Testament as a Whole

4C.19   NIELSEN, EDUARD. Oral Tradition: A Modern Problem in Old Testament Introduction. Studies in Biblical Theology, No. 11. London: SCM Press, 1954. 108 pp.
An advanced study of the oral tradition that underlies the written Old Testament.

4C.20   NORTH, C. R. "The Pentateuch," in 3B.3, pp. 35-39.
A brief background to the Pentateuch, including the theory of its composition.

4C.21   OESTERLEY, W. O. E., and THEODORE H. ROBINSON. An Introduction to the Books of the Old Testament. London: SPCK, 1958. 470 pp.
Pays special attention to metrical structure in the Prophets and devotes a separate chapter to "The Forms of Hebrew Poetry." Bibliography.

4C.22   PFEIFFER, ROBERT H. Introduction to the Old Testament. Revised edition. New York: Harper & Brothers, 1948. 921 pp.
Background on the Old Testament aimed at the nonspecialist. Liberally sprinkled with sections on the literary nature and value of parts of the Old Testament. Bibliography. Available in an abridged version, The Books of the Old Testament (1957).

4C.23   RAD, GERHARD VON. The Problem of the Hexateuch: And Other Essays. Translated by E. W. Trueman Dicken. New York: McGraw-Hill, 1966. 355 pp.
A collection of essays providing form-critical background on selected parts of the Bible. Of particular significance for the Bible as literature are "Some Aspects of the Old Testament Worldview" (pp. 144-165), providing a perspective on Old Testament thinking; "The Beginnings of Historical Writing in Ancient Israel" (pp. 166-204), contrasting Old Testament and modern concepts of history and storytelling; and the essays on Psalms, Job 38, and the Joseph narrative.

4C.24   ROBINSON, H[ENRY] WHEELER. The Old Testament: Its Making and Meaning. London: University of London Press, 1966. 258 pp.
A brief introduction to "the nature of the thirty-nine books which form our English Old Testament, together with their origins and dates...." Bibliography.

4C.25   ROWLEY, H[AROLD] H. The Growth of the Old Testament. London: Hutchinson University Library, 1950. 192 pp.
Discusses how the books of the Hebrew Bible came into existence and assumed their present form. A final section

4C   Introductions and Commentaries

discusses the growth and fixation of the canon. Admittedly presents "critical orthodoxy" to the reader. Short list of books for further reading.

4C.26   ROWLEY, H[AROLD] H. "The Literary Growth of the Old Testament," in 3B.3, pp. 28-34.
A brief account of the probable dates of the Old Testament books and how they were compiled. Reprinted in 3F.33, pp. 45-51.

4C.27   SANDMEL, SAMUEL. The Hebrew Scriptures: An Introduction to Their Literature and Religious Ideas. New York: Alfred A. Knopf, 1963.   588 pp.
Aims "to acquaint the reader ... with basic material that he will not have to unlearn." Chapters on each book of the Old Testament. Maps. Selected bibliography.

4C.28   SCHULTZ, SAMUEL J. The Old Testament Speaks. Second edition. New York: Harper & Row, 1970.   448 pp.
An introduction to the literature and history of the Old Testament for the general reader. Maps. Selected reading listed after each chapter.

4C.29   SOGGIN, J. ALBERTO. Introduction to the Old Testament: From Its Origins to the Closing of the Alexandrian Canon. The Old Testament Library. Philadelphia: Westminster Press, 1976. 544 pp.
Translation of an Italian work. Covers the Old Testament and deuterocanonical books. Includes discussions of myth, legend, history, and literary genres. Bibliography.

4C.30   WEST, JAMES KING. Introduction to the Old Testament: "Hear, O Israel." New York: Macmillan, 1971.   570 pp.
A college text covering the Old Testament and the Apocrypha. Maps, illustrations, and bibliography.

4D   The Literary Milieu of the Old Testament

See also 4A.6, 14; 4C.8, 10; 4I; 5B.6; 5I.11; 5L.16, 22, 38; 5M.5, 18; 50.1; 5P.3; 5U.3; 6.

4D.1   Anon. The Book of the Dead. Edited by E. A. Wallis Budge. New Hyde Park, New York: University Books, 1960.   720 pp.
Contains the hieroglyphic transcript of the Papyrus of Ani and an accompanying English translation of this important ancient Egyptian collection of hymns and prayers.

The Old Testament as a Whole

4D.2   Anon. The Epic of Gilgamesh: An English Version. Edited
by N. K. Sandars. Revised edition. Baltimore: Penguin Books,
1972. 128 pp.
A text edition of this well-known Sumerian epic, valuable
for the insights it provides on ancient mythology in general
and for the specific version of the Flood story it contains.
See 3L.10; 4D.9.

4D.3   BOWRA, C. M. Primitive Song. Cleveland: World Publishing
Company, 1962. 317 pp.
Studies the poetry of primitive peoples surviving today as
a means of learning about the earliest kinds of literature.
Background for the study of biblical poetry.

4D.4   DRIVER, GODFREY R. Canaanite Myths and Legends. Old Testament Studies, No. 3. Edinburgh: T & T Clark, 1956. 182 pp.
Transliteration and translation of the texts of these myths.
Introduction includes an analysis and interpretation of the
texts. Bibliography.

4D.5   FRANKFORT, H., H. A. FRANKFORT, JOHN A. WILSON, and THOR-
KILD JACOBSEN. Before Philosophy: The Intellectual Adventure
of Ancient Man. Baltimore: Penguin Books, 1946. 275 pp.
A study of the mythic thought patterns of the ancient peoples of Egypt and Mesopotamia. The final chapter shows "how
the Hebrews reduced the mythical element in their religion to
a minimum...."

4D.6   GAER, JOSEPH. The Lore of the Old Testament. Boston:
Little, Brown, 1951. 400 pp.
An introductory essay on the Bible in folk imagination is
followed by an extensive collection of Hebrew legends and folklore relating to Old Testament characters and events. Bibliography. See 7D.2.

4D.7   GRAY, JOHN. The Legacy of Canaan: The Ras Shamra Texts and
Their Relevance to the Old Testament. Supplements to Vetus
Testamentum, Vol. 5. Leiden: E. J. Brill, 1957. 253 pp.
An advanced study of ancient texts "documenting the life
and culture of Canaan on the eve of the Hebrew settlement."
Includes accounts of Canaanite myths, sagas, and legends, and
a study of literary and linguistic affinities with the Old
Testament. Bibliography.

4D.8   HEIDEL, ALEXANDER. The Babylonian Genesis: The Story of
Creation. Second edition. Chicago: University of Chicago
Press, 1951. 175 pp.

4D   The Literary Milieu

Translations of Enûma Elish and related Babylonian creation stories and an extensive discussion of Old Testament parallels. Companion to 4D.9. Photographs.

4D.9   HEIDEL, ALEXANDER. The Gilgamesh Epic and Old Testament Parallels. Second edition. Chicago: University of Chicago Press, 1949. 279 pp.
A translation of the epic and some related material and extensive discussion of themes and Old Testament parallels regarding death, the afterlife, and the flood. Companion to 4D.8. See 4D.2.

4D.10   PRITCHARD, JAMES B., ed. The Ancient Near East: An Anthology of Texts and Pictures. Princeton: Princeton University Press, 1958. 399 pp.
A collection of Near Eastern documents useful for providing a context for the Bible and a collection of photographs of ancient Near Eastern art objects. Material selected from 4A.19 and 4D.11.

4D.11   PRITCHARD, JAMES B., ed. Ancient Near Eastern Texts Relating to the Old Testament. Second edition. Princeton: Princeton University Press, 1955. 565 pp.
A collection of myths, rituals, laws, histories, and other documents from Israel's Near Eastern neighbors translated into modern English. See 4A.19 and 4D.10.

4D.12   THOMAS, D. WINTON, ed. Documents from Old Testament Times. London: Thomas Nelson & Sons, 1958. 328 pp.
Translations of ancient documents shedding light on the Old Testament from cuneiform, Egyptian, Moabite, Hebrew, and Aramaic sources. Introductions supply background for each document.

4D.13   WILLIAMS, RONALD J. "The Fable in the Ancient Near East," in A Stubborn Faith: Papers on Old Testament and Related Subjects. Edited by Edward C. Hobbs. Dallas: Southern Methodist University Press, 1956, pp. 3-26.
Surveys fable traditions in the ancient literatures of Egypt and the Near East that predate those of the Greek and Sanskrit collections. Cites examples from the Bible.

4E   The Old Testament as Literature: General Studies

See also 1B.10, 20; 3F; 5D.5-6.

4E.1   ACKERMAN, JAMES S., ALAN WILKIN JENKS, and EDWARD B. JENKINSON, with JAN BLOUGH. Teaching the Old Testament in English

Classes. Indiana University English Curriculum Study Series.
Bloomington: Indiana University Press, 1973. 511 pp.
Information about Old Testament background, the history of
Israel's literature, and ways of approaching Old Testament
narratives in literature classes. Includes discussion questions and bibliography. Replaces Ackerman's earlier On Teaching the Bible as Literature (1967).

4E.2   ACKERMAN, ROBERT, RUTH H. BLACKBURN, and UNICIO J. VIOLI.
Review Notes and Study Guide to the Old Testament. New York:
Monarch Press, 1964. 169 pp.
Introductory chapters on background followed by summaries
and commentaries on each book of the Old Testament and the
Apocrypha. Bibliography.

4E.3   ASIMOV, ISAAC. Asimov's Guide to the Bible. Volume 1: The
Old Testament. New York: Equinox Books (Avon), 1968. 716 pp.
A running commentary on people, places, and concepts as
they appear in the books of the Old Testament. "I am trying,
in short, to bring in the outside world, illuminate it in
terms of the biblical story and, in return, illuminate the
events of the Bible by adding to it the nonbiblical aspects of
history, biography, and geography." Written informally by the
famous science fiction author. Maps. See 7E.1.

4E.4   BEWER, JULIUS A. The Literature of the Old Testament.
Third edition, revised by Emil G. Kraeling. New York: Colum-
bia University Press, 1962. 511 pp.
A complete revision of a work first published in 1922.
Chapters arranged historically, starting with early poems and
narratives, leading into the Prophets and other writings, and
ending with Daniel and the Greek Peril. Selected bibliography.
See 7E.13.

4E.5   BLAND, KALMAN P. "The Rabbinic Method and Literary Criticism," in 3F.22, pp. 16-23.
To truly appreciate the Bible, we must read carefully and
consider hidden implications of every word and phrase. Illustrates this approach by discussing several examples from the
Pentateuch.

4E.6   CHASE, MARY ELLEN. Life and Language in the Old Testament.
New York: W. W. Norton, 1955. 201 pp.
Sequel to 3F.5, designed for a general audience. Background
discussions of the ancient Hebrew mind and the imagination and
language of the Old Testament. Brief bibliographical note.

4E.7   CULLEY, ROBERT C., ed. "Oral Tradition and Old Testament
Studies." Semeia, 5 (1976). 171 pp.

4E   General Studies

Articles and replies by several scholars. Contents: General
Studies: Robert C. Culley, "Oral Tradition and the OT: Some
Recent Discussion" (pp. 1-34); Burke O. Long, "Recent Field
Studies in Oral Literature and the Question of Sitz im Leben"
(pp. 35-50); Robert B. Coote, "The Application of Oral Theory
to Biblical Hebrew Literature" (pp. 51-64); Susan Wittig,
"Theories of Formulaic Narrative" (pp. 65-92); Critical Com-
ments (pp. 93-110); William J. Urbrock, "Oral Antecedents to
Job: A Survey of Formulas and Formulaic Systems" (pp. 111-138);
Discussion and Response (pp. 139-163).

4E.8   DRIVER, S[AMUEL] R. An Introduction to the Literature of
the Old Testament. Cleveland: World Publishing Company, 1956.
613 pp.
A classic scholarly study of the dates, authorship, and
literary form of the Old Testament books.

4E.9   GOOD, EDWIN M. "Ezekiel's Ship: Some Extended Metaphors in
the Old Testament." Semitics, 1 (1970), 79-103.
A discussion of several extended Old Testament metaphors
using I. A. Richards' "vehicle-tenor" concept.

4E.10   GOOD, EDWIN M. Irony in the Old Testament. Philadelphia:
Westminster Press, 1965. 256 pp.
A literary analysis focusing on irony in selected Old Testament books. Sandwiched between an introductory chapter and an
epilogue are essays on Jonah, Saul, Genesis, Isaiah, Qoheleth,
and Job. "I am inclined to think that the presence of irony
in the Old Testament casts a new light on the theological task
of interpretation."

4E.11   GUTHRIE, HARVEY H., JR. God and History in the Old Testament. Greenwich, Connecticut: Seabury Press, 1960. 189 pp.
A reading of the Old Testament emphasizing what its literature reveals about a philosophy of history and about its conception of God, "the chief character" of the work.
Bibliography.

4E.12   JAMES, FLEMING. Personalities of the Old Testament. New
York: Charles Scribner's Sons, 1951. 650 pp.
A study of the characters and writers of the Old Testament,
excluding the Psalmists. (See 5M.13.) Bibliography.

4E.13   MACDONALD, DUNCAN BLACK. The Hebrew Literary Genius: An
Interpretation Being an Introduction to the Reading of the Old
Testament. Princeton: Princeton University Press, 1933.
251 pp.

A loosely organized study of the Old Testament as literature. Argues that biblical scholars have lost sight of the
forest for the trees; the time has come to concern ourselves
again with the overall effect of the biblical stories. In a
companion volume, The Hebrew Philosophical Genius (1936), Mac-
Donald expands his studies of Hebrew philosophy and of Ecclesiastes. *Reprinted: New York: Russell & Russell, 1968
(cited in 3M.17).

4E.14   MOORE, GEORGE FOOT. The Literature of the Old Testament.
New York: Henry Holt, 1913. 256 pp.
    An early study of the Old Testament as a national litera-
ture. Concentrates largely--though not exclusively--on the
history of the text. Bibliography.

4E.15   MUILENBURG, JAMES. "A Study in Hebrew Rhetoric: Repetition
and Style." Congress Volume (Supplements to Vetus Testamentum,
vol. 1). Leiden: E. J. Brill, 1953, pp. 97-111.
    An advanced study of repetition as a stylistic device in
ancient Hebrew literature.

4E.16   MYERS, FRANKLIN G. The Old Testament. Barnes & Noble
Book Notes. New York: Barnes & Noble, 1968. 93 pp.
    Contains summaries and brief discussions of each Old Testa-
ment book. Bibliography.

4E.17   OHLSEN, WOODROW. Perspectives on Old Testament Literature.
New York: Harcourt Brace Jovanovich, 1978. 463 pp.
    Emphasizes a truly literary approach. Nineteen Old Testa-
ment books are summarized; each is followed by selections from
major critics and commentators who address the literary qualities and the various interpretations of the book. Designed as
a supplementary text for college literature courses. Maps and
photographs. Each chapter concludes with a list of suggested
readings.

4E.18   PATTERSON, CHARLES H. The Old Testament: Notes. Lincoln,
Nebraska: Cliffs Notes, 1965. 96 pp.
    Summaries and brief commentaries on the books.
Bibliography.

4E.19   PAYNE, D. F. "A Perspective on the Use of Simile in the
Old Testament." Semitics, 1 (1970), 111-125.
    A study of simile--as distinct from metaphor--in the Old
Testament.

4E.20   POWYS, JOHN COWPER. "The Bible as Literature: The Old
Testament," in his Enjoyment of Literature. New York: Simon &
Schuster, 1938, pp. 3-34.

4E   General Studies

Inspired by the appearance of 1B.5. Defends the value of the Old Testament as literature in the spirit of older, romantic criticism. Reprinted in 3F.33, pp. 185-208.

4E.21   PRIEST, JOHN F. "Humanism, Scepticism, and Pessimism in Israel." Journal of the American Academy of Religion, 36 (1968), 311-326.
An argues that the Old Testament takes a human perspective on life and thus illustrates humanism, scepticism, and pessimism in action. Particular reference to scepticism in Job and Ecclesiastes.

4E.22   ROBERTSON, DAVID. The Old Testament and the Literary Critic. Guides to Biblical Scholarship, Old Testament Series. Philadelphia: Fortress Press, 1977. 95 pp.
Essays by a scholar trained in both biblical studies and contemporary literary criticism. An introductory chapter on the nature of a literary study of the Bible is followed by specific treatments of Exodus, Job, Psalm 90 (reprinted in 5M.21), and the Prophets. Bibliography.

4E.23   ROSNER, DOV. "The Simile and Its Use in the Old Testament." Semitics, 4 (1974), 37-46.
An advanced study of the use and purpose of "the two main types of simile in the Old Testament."

4E.24   SANDMEL, SAMUEL. The Enjoyment of Scripture: The Law, the Prophets, and the Writings. New York: Oxford University Press, 1972. 314 pp.
A noted biblical scholar presents a literary analysis of the Old Testament. "Whatever else the Hebrews were, they were pre-eminently a race of extraordinarily gifted writers." Bibliography.

4E.25   TRAWICK, BUCKNER B. The Bible as Literature: The Old Testament and the Apocrypha. Second edition. New York: Barnes & Noble, 1970. 410 pp.
An outline of, and commentary on, each book of the Old Testament and the Apocrypha from a literary perspective. Supersedes The Bible as Literature: Old Testament History and Biography. (Barnes & Noble, 1963). See 3D.9 and 7E.15.

4E.26   VAN DOREN, MARK, and MAURICE SAMUEL. In the Beginning, Love: Dialogues on the Bible. Edited by Edith Samuel. New York: John Day Company, 1973. 288 pp.
Fifteen conversations (in dialogue form), originally broadcast on radio by two men of letters. Informal observations on the theme of love in many parts of the Old Testament and the book of Tobit, several taking a literary perspective. See 5M.25.

4E.27   WILLIAMS, JAY G. <u>Understanding the Old Testament</u>. Woodbury, New York: Barron's Educational Series, 1972. 350 pp.
     An introductory text for the nonspecialist, emphasizing the
"literature, history, impact on Western culture, and relevance
to our contemporary society" of the Old Testament. Introductory chapters are followed by summaries and commentaries on
each of the thirty-nine books. Bibliography. <u>See</u> 3D.9.

4F   The Old Testament as Literature: Narrative

See also 3A.13; 3G; 4A.15; 4C.23; 4E.1; 5A.1, 5; 5H.2; 5I.1, 6-7, 11.

4F.1   ADAR, ZVI. <u>The Biblical Narrative</u>. Translated by Misha
Louvish. Jerusalem: Department of Education and Culture of
the World Zionist Organization, 1959. 280 pp.
     A study of selected isolated folktales in the Hebrew Bible
and their integration into the larger framework of the complete biblical narrative. Chapters consider the successive
stages experienced by a tale as it becomes incorporated into
this framework.

4F.2   CHURCH, BROOKE PETERS. <u>The Golden Years: The Old Testament
Narrative as Literature</u>. New York: Rinehart, 1947. 408 pp.
     Surveys "the literary method of Hebrew narrative writing
and . . . its results." Treats the major narrative sections
of the Hebrew Bible (and the Book of Tobit) as separate units.
Reprints the texts of the early narratives (in the King James
Translation) in "the version of the Seventh Century B.C., in
so far as it can be recovered." Pp. 21-53 (on the stories of
David and the Hebrew concept of history) reprinted in 3F.33,
pp. 237-270.

4F.3   CHURCH, BROOKE PETERS. <u>The Israel Saga</u>. Foreword by
Charles C. Torrey. New York: Macmillan, 1932, 341 pp.
     An earlier study of Old Testament narrative as literature.
Covers material through Kings with brief treatments of later
work. Bibliography.

4F.4   CULLEY, ROBERT C., ed. "Classical Hebrew Narrative."
<u>Semeia</u>, 3 (1975). 156 pp.
     Articles and replies by different scholars on biblical nar-
rative. Contents: Robert C. Culley, "Themes and Variations in
Three Groups of OT Narratives" (pp. 3-13); David M. Gunn,
"David and the Gift of the Kingdom (2 Sam. 2-4, 9-20, 1 Kgs.
1-2)" (pp. 14-45); Burke O. Long, "The Social Setting for Prophetic Miracle Stories" (pp. 46-63); Sean E. McEvenue, "A Comparison of Narrative Styles in the Hagar Stories" (pp. 64-80);

4F Narrative

Robert Polzin, "'The Ancestress of Israel in Danger' in Danger" (pp. 81-98); Hugh C. White, "French Structuralism and OT Narrative Analysis: Roland Barthes" (pp. 99-127); Critical Comments (pp. 128-148).

4F.5   CULLEY, ROBERT C. Studies in the Structure of Hebrew Narrative. Semeia Supplements. Philadelphia: Fortress Press, 1976. 128 pp.
A monograph studying the oral transmission of prose in general, its relevance to selected Old Testament texts, and its implications for a study of structure in biblical stories of miraculous happenings. Bibliography.

4F.6   MALAMAT, ABRAHAM. "The Danite Migration and the Pan-Israelite Exodus-Conquest: A Biblical Narrative Pattern." Biblica, 51 (1970), 1-16.
Sees a common narrative pattern in the Danite migration (Judges 18) and the large-scale Exodus and Conquest stories in the Pentateuch.

4F.7   WILDER, AMOS N. "Biblical Epos and Modern Narrative," in his The New Voice: Religion, Literature, Hermeneutics. New York: Herder and Herder, 1969, pp. 41-77, passim.
Comments on various stylistic features of Old Testament epic narrative citing parallels in modern literature.

4G The Old Testament as Literature: Poetry and Poetics

See also 3E.10, 12, 18; 3H; 4A.15; 4B.11; 4C.21; 4D.3; 4I.7; 4K.1; 5B.1; 5D.7; 5E.1-2; 5G.3; 5I.6; 5L.3, 23; 5M.8, 11-12, 24; 5Q.1.

4G.1   GEVIRTZ, STANLEY. Patterns in the Early Poetry of Israel. Studies in Ancient Oriental Civilization, No. 32. Chicago: University of Chicago Press, 1963. 107 pp.
An advanced monograph on parallelism with specific studies of the eulogy of Saul and David (1 Samuel 18:7); Lamech's Song (Genesis 4:23-24); Isaac's Blessing (Genesis 27:28-29); Balaam's first "Mashal" (Numbers 23:7-10); and David's Lament (2 Samuel 1:18-27).

4G.2   GLÜCK, J. J. "Assonance in Ancient Hebrew Poetry: Sound Patterns as a Literary Device," in De Fructu Oris Sui: Essays in Honor of Adrianus van Selms. Edited by I. H. Eybers, et al. Pretoria Oriental Series, No. 9. Leiden: E. J. Brill, 1971, pp. 69-84.
Studies the use of sounds in biblical poetry. "Assonance occurs everywhere in the Old Testament, both in the poetry and in the prose sections, and it is invariably appropriate."

4G.3   KRAFT, CHARLES F. "Some Further Observations concerning the Strophic Structure of Hebrew Poetry," in <u>A Stubborn Faith</u>: <u>Papers on Old Testament and Related Subjects</u>. Edited by Edward C. Hobbs. Dallas: Southern Methodist University Press, 1956, pp. 62–89.
A study of the larger units within biblical poems. Strophic structure enhances both the beauty and meaning of the poetry and should be reflected when poems are printed in modern translations.

4G.4   MONTGOMERY, JAMES A. "Stanza-Formation in Hebrew Poetry." <u>Journal of Biblical Literature</u>, 64 (1945), 379–384.
Studies the stanzaic structure of the Psalms and other biblical poems.

4G.5   ROBINSON, THEODORE H. <u>The Poetry of the Old Testament</u>. London: Gerald Duckworth, 1947. 231 pp.
Studies the poetry as literature. Brief treatment of isolated poems and more extensive coverage of Job, Psalms, Proverbs, Song of Songs, and Lamentations. Bibliography.

4G.6   WHALLON, WILLIAM. <u>Formula, Character, and Context: Studies in Homeric, Old English, and Old Testament Poetry</u>. Cambridge, Massachusetts: Harvard University Press, 1969. 241 pp.
A comparative study of verbal formulas in relation to characterization and context. The last two chapters (pp. 139–210) discuss word pairs, hemistichs and distichs in Old Testament poetry, and the relation of the poetry to the prose. Brief consideration of Jesus as a poet.

4G.7   WHALLON, WILLIAM, "Formulaic Poetry in the Old Testament." <u>Comparative Literature</u>, 15 (1963), 1–14.
An advanced study arguing that "Hebraic synonymy was a prosodic device analogous to the Homeric epithet and the Anglo-Saxon kenning."

4G.8   WHALLON, WILLIAM. "Old Testament Poetry and Homeric Epic." <u>Comparative Literature</u>, 18 (1966), 113–131.
Criticizes Auerbach's comparison between the <u>Odyssey</u> and Genesis 22 (<u>See</u> 5C.1). Auerbach unjustifiably compared Homeric poetry with biblical prose; he ignored biblical poetry. "On the basis of style, the Hebraic mind or world view cannot be distinguished from the intelligence behind the <u>Odyssey</u> or <u>Iliad</u>."

4H   The Old Testament as Literature: Apocalyptic Literature

4H Apocalyptic Literature

See also 8J.8, 10.

4H.1   FROST, STANLEY BRICE. Old Testament Apocalyptic: Its Origins and Growth. London: Epworth Press, 1952. 283 pp.
     A study of the nature and development of apocalyptic writings in the Old Testament.

4H.2   HANSON, PAUL D. The Dawn of Apocalyptic. Philadelphia: Fortress Press, 1975. 438 pp.
     An advanced study of apocalyptic elements in Isaiah, Ezekiel, Haggai, and Zechariah. Bibliography.

4H.3   RUSSEL, D. S. The Method and Message of Jewish Apocalpytic: 200 B.C. - A.D. 100. Old Testament Library. Philadelphia: Westminster Press, 1964. 464 pp.
     Covers the nature, techniques, and major themes of this literature, which is seen as the work of "visionaries and poets." Bibliography.

4H.4   WILDER, AMOS N. "The Rhetoric of Ancient and Modern Apocalyptic." Interpretation, 25 (1971), 436-453.
     Attempts to describe the nature of apocalyptic utterance in its earliest phases. Does not analyze specific texts at length, but provides theoretical background on the nature of this kind of writing.

4I The Old Testament as Literature: Myth and Legend

See also 3E.19; 3J; 4C.29; 4D; 5A.2-3; 5B; 5C.2, 9; 5I.9; 5L.22, 24, 38; 5U.3.

4I.1   BUBER, MARTIN. "Saga and History." Chapter 1 of his Moses: The Revelation and the Covenant. New York: Harper & Row, 1958, pp. 13-19.
     As a prologue to his attempt in this book to demonstrate that Moses was a historical personage, the noted Jewish philosopher distinguishes between saga and history in general.

4I.2   CHILDS, BREVARD S. Myth and Reality in the Old Testament. Second edition. Studies in Biblical Theology, No. 27. London: SCM Press, 1962. 112 pp.
     The nature and role of myth and its evolving conflict with the Old Testament concept of "reality." Specific discussions of selected passages from Genesis, Exodus, and Isaiah.

4I.3   CROSS, FRANK MOORE. Canaanite Myth and Hebrew Epic: Essays in the History of the Religion of Israel. Cambridge, Massachusetts: Harvard University Press, 1973. 394 pp.

An advanced study of the continued tension between the mythic and the historic in Israelite history. Sees Israelite religious expression assuming the form of the epic.

4I.4   FRAZER, JAMES GORDON.   Folk-Lore in the Old Testament: Studies in Comparative Religion, Legend, and Law.   Three volumes.   London: Macmillan, 1918.   Volume 1, 594 pp.; volume 2, 593 pp.; volume 3, 584 pp.
A study of superstitions and legends depicted in the Bible which may have survived from earlier periods of Hebrew history. Compares elements of Hebrew folklore to folklore of other cultures.   See 4I.6.

4I.5   FROMM, ERICH.   The Forgotten Language: An Introduction to the Understanding of Dreams, Fairy Tales, and Myths.   New York: Holt, Rinehart & Winston, 1951.   270 pp.
A psychologist's introduction to an understanding of symbolic language.   Included are brief discussions of the stories of Jonah (pp. 20-23), Pharaoh's dreams (pp. 111-114), and the Sabbath ritual (pp. 241-249), along with analyses of myths from other cultures.

4I.6   GASTER, THEODOR H.   Myth, Legend, and Custom in the Old Testament: A Comparative Study with Chapters from Sir James G. Frazer's Folklore in the Old Testament.   New York: Harper & Row, 1969.   954 pp.
An expansion of 4I.4.   Episodes in the Old Testament are discussed as myth and compared with similar myths from other cultures.

4I.7   GASTER, THEODOR H.   Thespis: Ritual, Myth, and Drama in the Ancient Near East.   Revised edition.   Garden City, New York: Doubleday, 1961.   515 pp.
A study of seasonal drama myths in Canaanite, Hittite, Egyptian, and Hebrew literature.   Includes a chapter on "Survivals in Biblical and Classical Poetry."   Bibliography.

4I.8   GINZBERG, LOUIS.   The Legends of the Jews.   Seven volumes. Philadelphia: Jewish Publication Society of America, 1946-1961.
"A collection of Jewish legends that deal with Biblical personages and events."   A one-volume abridgement, Legends of the Bible (1975), is available.

4I.9   KAUFMAN, U. MILO.   "Expostulation with the Divine: A Note on Contrasting Attitudes in Greek and Hebrew Piety."   Interpretation, 18 (1964), 171-182.
Argues that the Greeks and Hebrews differed in the degree to which they expostulated with their deities.   Contrasts Job to Oedipus, and Moses to Orestes.   Reprinted in 5L.36.

The Old Testament as a Whole

4I Myth and Legend

4I.10   KLUGER, RIVKAH SCHÄRF. Satan in the Old Testament. Translated by Hildegard Nagel. Evanston, Illinois: Northwestern
University Press, 1967. 191 pp.
     A Jungian reading of the development of Satan as an indi-
vidual character in the Old Testament. Satan is seen arche-
typally as "the symbolic expression of certain aspects of
man's inner spiritual reality."

4I.11   LEACH, MARIA. The Beginning: Creation Myths around the
World. New York: Funk & Wagnalls, 1956. 253 pp.
     A collection from both the Old and New Worlds. Illustra-
tions and bibliography.

4I.12   SHARPLESS, F. PARVIN. The Myth of the Fall: Literature of
Innocence and Experience. Hayden Humanities Series. Rochelle
Park, New Jersey: Hayden Book Company, 1974. 250 pp.
     An anthology of English and American literature on the
theme. Includes a seventeen-page introduction on the meaning
of the myth, and reprints selections from Genesis in both the
King James and New English versions. A student text.

4I.13   WILCOXEN, JAY A. "Some Anthropocentric Aspects of Israel's
Sacred History." Journal of Religion, 48 (1968), 333-350.
     Studies the mythlike nature of the Old Testament sacred
history, focusing on the theme of Israel's wandering in the
Wilderness. The history suggests by analogy the stages in
the development of a man's life.

4J The Old Testament as Literature: Language and Linguistics

See also 3K; 4D.7; 5A.9; 5B.3-4; 5D.1; 5L.20; 5M.24-25.

4J.1   BARR, JAMES. "The Nature of Linguistic Evidence in the
Text of the Bible," in Language and Texts: The Nature of Linguistic Evidence. Edited by Herbert H. Paper. Ann Arbor,
Michigan: Center for Coordination of Ancient and Modern Studies, University of Michigan, 1975, pp. 35-57.
     An advanced study of the Hebrew Old Testament, investigat-
ing linguistic evidence as evidence of the language itself and
as a guide to interpretation.

4J.2   THOMAS, D. WINTON. "The Language of the Old Testament,"
in 3B.3, pp. 1-5.
     A brief description of the Old Testament languages, Hebrew
and Aramaic, for the layman.

The Old Testament as a Whole

4K   The Old Testament as Literature: Structuralism

See also 3K.L; 4F.4, 5; 5A.1; 5B.2; 5C.4; 5I.9; 5L.30.

4K.1   AP-ROBERTS, RUTH.   "Old Testament Poetry: The Translatable
        Structure." PMLA, 92 (1977), 987-1003.
            Old Testament poetry is particularly translatable because
        of its reliance on parallelism: the "rhyming" of ideas. This
        phenomenon has implications for structuralist studies.

5 The Old Testament: Individual Books

5A   Genesis: General Studies

See also 3J.15; 4E.10; 4I.1; 5B-C; 5D.1.

5A.1   FOKKELMAN, J. P. Narrative Art in Genesis: Specimens of
          Stylistic and Structural Analysis. Amsterdam: Van Gorcum
          Assen, 1975. 244 pp.
             An advanced study of the Tower of Babel story and of selec-
          ted stories about Jacob treated as literature. Uses the
          structuralist approach. Bibliography.

5A.2   GRAVES, ROBERT, and RAPHAEL PATAI. Hebrew Myths: The Book
          of Genesis. Garden City, New York: Doubleday, 1964. 311 pp.
             A companion to Graves's The Greek Myths, similarly organ-
          ized. Various accounts of the Genesis myths--from other
          sources and traditions as well as from Scripture--are followed
          by lengthy explanatory notes. Annotated bibliography.

5A.3   GUNKEL, HERMANN. The Legends of Genesis: The Biblical Saga
          and History. Translated by W. H. Carruth. New York: Schocken
          Books, 1964. 178 pp.
             The opening section of his Commentary on Genesis (1901).
          Studies the nature and development of the legends and con-
          cludes that they reflect a good deal of historical fact. Form-
          critical observations on the original functions of the stories.

5A.4   LEIBOWITZ, NEHAMA. Studies in Bereshit (Genesis): In the
          Context of Ancient and Modern Jewish Bible Commentary. Trans-
          lated and adapted by Aryeh Newman. Third revised edition.
          Jerusalem: World Zionist Organization, 1976. 656 pp.
             A commentary by a modern Jewish scholar incorporating views
          of other such scholars through the ages. An earlier edition
          was called Studies in the Book of Genesis.

5A.5   MCEVENUE, SEAN E. The Narrative Style of the Priestly
          Writer. Analecta Biblica, No. 50. Rome: Biblical Institute
          Press, 1971. 230 pp.

5A   Genesis: General Studies

A literary analysis studying the style of the Pentateuch writer identified as P. Examines the style in relation to children's literature. Specific, detailed analyses of the Flood story, the spy story of Numbers 13–14, and the oath to Abraham (Genesis 17). Bibliography.

5A.6   RAD, GERHARD VON. Genesis: A Commentary. Translated by John H. Marks. The Old Testament Library. Philadelphia: Westminster Press, 1961. 434 pp.
A line-by-line commentary with the passages from the Revised Standard Version of Genesis followed by discussion. "A great deal of effort has been expended to give the reader as clear an idea as possible of the kind of literature with which he is dealing in each instance."

5A.7   SPEISER, E. A. Genesis. The Anchor Bible, 1. Garden City, New York: Doubleday, 1964. 455 pp.
See 1A.1 and 4C.7.

5A.8   VAWTER, BRUCE. On Genesis: A New Reading. Garden City, New York: Doubleday, 1977. 501 pp.
A passage-by-passage commentary based on the Roman Catholic New American Bible.

5A.9   WILSON, EDMUND. "On First Reading Genesis," in his Red, Black, Blond, and Olive: Studies in Four Civilizations. New York: Oxford University Press, 1956, pp. 387–426.
Informal account of Wilson's first venture through Genesis after acquiring a smattering of Hebrew. Discusses the nature of the language and the non-Western world view suggested by the episodes of the book.

5B   Genesis: The Myths (Chapters 1–11)

See also 3A.4; 3E.11; 3F.1, 17; 3J.17; 3M.8; 4D.4, 8–9; 4G.1; 4I.5, 11–12; 5A; 5U.3.

5B.1   ANDERSON, BERNHARD W. Creation versus Chaos: The Reinterpretation of Mythical Symbolism in the Bible. New York: Association Press, 1967. 192 pp.
Studies the poetic use of the mythical conflict between the Creator and chaos in the Bible. Bibliography.

5B.2   ANDERSON, BERNHARD W. "From Aanlysis to Synthesis: The Interpretation of Genesis 1–11." Journal of Biblical Literature, 97 (1978), 23–39.

Surveys the major critical stances of the twentieth century
and summarizes past analysis of the Flood story. Analyzes the
structural and stylistic features that make the story a dramatic unity. The story moves "from the original harmony of
creation, through the violent disruption of that order and
the near return to chaos, and finally to a new creation. . . ."

5B.3   BURKE, KENNETH. "On the First Three Chapters of Genesis."
       Daedalus, 87, no. 3 (1958), 37-64.
          Compares the "rectilinear" style of the Genesis narrative
       with the "cycle of terms" associated with the idea of Order.
       Logologically, the narrative provides a new slant on the mean-
       ing of death. See 5B.4. Reprinted in Symbolism in Religion
       and Literature. Edited by Rollo May. New York: George Bra-
       ziller, 1960, pp. 118-151.

5B.4   BURKE, KENNETH. The Rhetoric of Religion: Studies in Logo-
       logy. Boston: Beacon Press, 1961. 335 pp.
          This study of the relationship between theology and lang-
       uage includes an extended analysis of the Creation and Fall
       (Genesis 1-3). "The essay shows the ways whereby the idea of
       order as stated narratively, tautologically implies the idea
       of original sin . . . and . . . how the idea of original sin
       in turn tautologically implies the idea of redemption. . . ."
       This essay is an expansion of 5B.3.

5B.5   GONEN, JAY Y. "Then Men Said, 'Let Us Make God in Our
       Image, after Our Likeness.'" Literature and Psychology, 21
       (1971), 69-79.
          A psychological study of the Creation story as "a projec-
       tion of man's image of himself not only as he is, but as he
       would like to be."

5B.6   GRAVES, ROBERT. Adam's Rib and Other Anomalous Elements in
       the Hebrew Creation Myth. With wood engravings by James Met-
       calf. London: Trianon Press, 1955. 73 pp.
          Argues that the Genesis Creation story results from a post-
       Exilic priest's misreading of ancient icons from Hebron and
       his attempts to combine these with Israelite and Babylonian
       legends to produce a workable monotheistic creation story.
       Text and engravings present the argument, the Genesis version
       of the icon's story, and a hypothetical reconstruction of the
       original version of the story.

5B.7   GROS LOUIS, KENNETH R. R. "The Garden of Eden," in 3F.22,
       pp. 52-58.
          Argues for a reading of Adam and Eve as full-grown, perfect
       beings--not children--before the Fall. Their story reflects

5B Genesis: The Myths

> universal patterns of temptation, evil, and guilt, regardless
> of its historical validity. "The narrative seems to explore
> sin in its many manifestations."

5B.8   GROS LOUIS, KENNETH R. R. "Genesis 1-2," in 3F.22, pp. 41-
        51.
        The two accounts of Creation in these chapters provide com-
plementary, not contradictory, views of God: as the distant,
all-powerful Creator, and as the immanent, concerned Father.

5B.9   RALSTON, WILLIAM H., JR. "That Old Serpent (for C. T. H.)."
        Sewanee Review, 81 (1973), 389-428.
        A reading of Genesis 1-3 as literature, emphasizing the
mythological foundations of the passage and identifying the
primordial chaos of Genesis 1:2 as a central image.

5B.10   WESTERMANN, CLAUS. The Genesis Accounts of Creation.
        Translated by Norman E. Wagner. Facet Books Biblical Series,
        No. 7. Philadelphia: Fortress Press, 1964. 48 pp.
        A reading of Genesis 1-3, emphasizing what the text says
over any preconceptions we might bring to it. Presents the
"several source theory." Bibliography.

5C Genesis: The Patriarchs (Chapters 12-50)

See also 3A.4; 3D.1; 3F.1; 3G.8; 3L.5; 3M.8; 4A.8; 4C.23; 4F.4; 4G.1;
4I.5; 5A; 5H.6; 5I.11.

5C.1   AUERBACH, ERICH. "Odysseus' Scar," in his Mimesis: The Re-
        presentation of Reality in Western Literature. Translated by
        Willard R. Trask. Princeton: Princeton University Press, 1953,
        pp. 3-23.
        A study of the contrasts between the literary styles of
Homer and the Old Testament writers, focusing on the Genesis
account of the sacrifice of Isaac (Genesis 22). Unlike Homer,
Hebrew writers generally left such things as time, place, and
feeling unexpressed in their narratives. Biblical characters
developed and changed (compare the young and old Jacob), while
Homeric characters did not (compare the young and old Odysseus). See 3F.45 and 4G.8. Reprinted in 3F.33, pp. 209-230.

5C.2   BOOTH, A. PETER. "Abraham and Agamemnon: A Study of Myth."
        Humanities Association Review, 25 (1974), 290-297.
        A comparison of Agamemnon's sacrifice of Iphigenia and
Abraham's near-sacrifice of Isaac.

5C   Genesis: The Patriarchs

5C.3   CLEMENTS, R. E. Abraham and David: Genesis 15 and Its Mean-
ing for Israelite Tradition. Studies in Biblical Theology.
Second Series, No. 5. London: SCM Press, 1967. 96 pp.
Historical and theological background on the role of the
Abrahamic covenant (Genesis 15) in Israel's life.
Bibliography.

5C.4   CRENSHAW, JAMES. "Journey into Oblivion: A Structural
Analysis of Genesis 22:1-19." Soundings, 58 (1975), 243-256.
Analyzes the story of Abraham's sacrifice of Isaac, relating it to other biblical accounts of a son sacrificed by a
father. Reprinted in 3L.10.

5C.5   FRITSCH, CHARLES T. "'God Was with Him': A Theological
Study of the Joseph Narrative." Interpretation, 9 (1955),
21-34.
Despite its subtitle this article also deals substantially
with the literary qualities of the Joseph story (Genesis 37-
50).

5C.6   KIERKEGAARD, SØREN. "Fear and Trembling," in Fear and
Trembling and The Sickness unto Death. Translated by Walter
Lowrie. An Anchor Book. Garden City, New York: Doubleday,
1954, pp. 21-132.
Contains a reading of the story of Abraham's sacrifice of
Isaac in Genesis. A difficult philosophical treatise using
this story as a basis for examining the nature of faith.

5C.7   REDFORD, DONALD B. A Study of the Biblical Story of Joseph.
Supplements to Vetus Testamentum, Vol. 20. Leiden: E. J.
Brill, 1970. 304 pp.
Studies several aspects of Genesis 37-50; includes a section on "The Joseph Story as Literature" (pp. 66-105) with
comments on plot symmetry, irony, motifs, and other literary
elements. Bibliography.

5C.8   SEYBOLD, DONALD A. "Paradox and Symmetry in the Joseph
Narrative," in 3F.22, pp. 59-73.
A formalist literary analysis of the Joseph story. "This
analysis makes very clear the literary forms of repetition,
pattern, and character that operate in the story and give it
an elegance and eloquence quite apart from its religious, historical, or theological significance."

5C.9   SHOHAM, S. GIORA. "The Isaac Syndrome." American Imago,
33 (1976), 329-349.
A psychoanalytical reading of the sacrifice of Isaac as an
archetypal depiction of "the normative pressures directed from

5D   Exodus (Including Moses)

father to son."   "The myth of the offering of Isaac may,
therefore, be taken in its psychological context as a basic
family dynamic which counteracts the oedipal pressures postu-
lated by Freud."

5D   Exodus (Including Moses)

See also 2C.7; 3A.4; 3J.16; 4A.21; 4E.22; 4F.6; 4I.1, 9; 5S.4;
8G.5, 8.

5D.1   ACKERMAN, JAMES S.   "The Literary Context of the Moses
Birth Story," in 3F.22, pp. 74-119.
A close reading of Exodus 1-2, suggesting that this central
passage reflects back to the language and themes of Genesis
and looks ahead to the major themes of the rest of Exodus:
Egypt, waters, and wilderness.

5D.2   BARZEL, HILLEL.   "Moses: Tragedy and Sublimity," in 3F.22,
pp. 120-140.
Considers tragedy and sublimity as they relate to the Old
Testament generally and then applies them specifically to the
figure of Moses.

5D.3   CHRISTEN, ROBERT J., and HAROLD E. HAZELTON.   Monotheism
and Moses.   Problems in European Civilization.   Lexington,
Massachusetts: D. C. Heath, 1969.   122 pp.
A source book of selections providing different viewpoints
on Moses and his role as Hebrew leader.   Useful for background
on Moses.   Bibliography.

5D.4   DAICHES, DAVID.   Moses: The Man and His Vision.   New York:
Praeger, 1975.   264 pp.
A reading of the Moses story by a famous literary critic.
Illustrations.

5D.5   DAUBE, DAVID.   The Exodus Pattern in the Bible.   All Souls
Studies, No. 2.   London: Faber & Faber, 1963.   94 pp.
A study of the motif of exodus throughout the Bible.

5D.6   DOWNING, CHRISTINE.   "How Can We Hope and Not Dream?   Exodus as Metaphor: A Study of the Biblical Imagination."   Journal
of Religion, 48 (1968), 35-53.
Traces the development of the metaphor of exodus through
much of the Old Testament and argues for reading the Old Testament metaphorically.

5D   Exodus (Including Moses)

5D.7   FREEDMAN, DAVID NOEL. "Strophe and Meter in Exodus 15," in A Light unto My Path: Old Testament Studies in Honor of Jacob M. Myers. Edited by Howard N. Bream, Ralph D. Heim, and Carey A. Moore. Philadelphia: Temple University Press, 1974, pp. 163–203.
         An advanced metrical analysis of this poem, delineating its strophic structure. Includes detailed textual and interpretive notes on each verse.

5D.8   FREUD, SIGMUND. Moses and Monotheism. Translated by Katharine Jones. Hogarth Press, 1939. 223 pp.
         Background to the biblical stories of Moses. The famous psychoanalyst presents his theory that Moses was an Egyptian and explains the rise of the Jewish people and their religion on this basis.

5D.9   GASTER, THEODOR HERZL. Passover: Its History and Traditions. Boston: Beacon Press, 1962. 102 pp.
         Attempts "to tell the story of the festival . . . against the background of modern knowledge." Provides a context for Exodus and includes a chapter on "Folklore in the Bible Story." Bibliography.

5D.10   LEIBOWITZ, NEHAMA. Studies in Shemot (The Book of Exodus). Two volumes. Translated and adapted by Aryeh Newman. Jerusalem: World Zionist Organization, 1976. 799 pp.
         A commentary by a modern Jewish scholar which incorporates comments from other major Jewish scholars.

5D.11   LUKER, MAURICE SYLVESTER, JR. "The Figure of Moses in the Plague Traditions." Ph.D. dissertation, Drew University, 1968. Abstracted in Dissertation Abstracts, 29 (1968), 1283A.
         Analyzes the pictures of Moses in the Plague narratives (Exodus 7:8–10:27).

5D.12   MCEVENUE, SEAN. "The Style of a Building Instruction." Semitics, 4 (1974), 1–9.
         Studies the style of Exodus 25:31–40.

5D.13   NOTH, MARTIN. Exodus: A Commentary. Translated by J. S. Bowden. The Old Testament Library. Philadelphia: Westminster Press, 1962. 283 pp.
         A line-by-line commentary: passages from the Revised Standard Version Exodus followed by discussions.

5D.14   ZELIGS, DOROTHY F. "The Family Romance of Moses." American Imago, 23 (1966), 110–131.

5E Leviticus-Numbers-Deuteronomy

> Together with two sequels--"Moses in Midian: The Burning
> Bush," American Imago, 26 (1969), 379-400; "Moses Encounters
> the Daemonic Aspect of God," American Imago, 27 (1970), 379-
> 391--presents a psychoanalytical reading of Moses' maturation
> as revealed in Exodus. "Moses came to Midian as a youth in
> the throes of a crisis in self-identity. He returned to Egypt
> as a leader of phenomenal strength and resolution."

5E Leviticus - Numbers - Deuteronomy

See also 4A.21; 4B.11; 4G.1; 5A.5; 5N.1; 5S.4; 8I.19.

5E.1   BOSTON, JAMES R. "The Wisdom Influence upon the Song of
Moses." Journal of Biblical Literature, 87 (1968), 198-202.
    Argues for a definite relationship between this song (Deu-
teronomy 32:1-43) and the Wisdom tradition.

5E.2   LABUSCHAGNE, C. J. "The Song of Moses: Its Framework and
Structure," in De Fructu Oris Sui: Essays in Honor of Adrianus
van Selms. Edited by I. H. Eybers, et al. Pretoria Oriental
Series, No. 9. Leiden: E. J. Brill, 1971, pp. 85-98.
    Studies the context, form, and substance of Deuteronomy 32.

5F Joshua

See 4A.11, 21.

5G Judges

See also 4A.11; 4B.1; 4F.6.

5G.1   BLENKINSOPP, J. "Structure and Style in Judges 13-16."
Journal of Biblical Literature, 82 (1963), 65-76.
    A literary analysis of the Samson cycle. "The view is
taken here . . . that the expositor should have the habit of
looking at the passage as a whole, while having an acute
awareness of its literary history."

5G.2   BOLING, ROBERT G. Judges. The Anchor Bible, 6A. Garden
City, New York: Doubleday, 1975. 360 pp.
    See 1A.1.

5G.3   GLOBE, ALEXANDER. "The Literary Structure and Unity of the
Song of Deborah." Journal of Biblical Literature, 93 (1974),
493-512.
    An advanced study of Judges 5 as literature.

5G.4   GROS LOUIS, KENNETH R. R. "The Book of Judges," in 3F.22, pp. 141-162.
Considers the book as a unified whole, with its own themes and structures, rather than as a collection of isolated incidents.

5H   Ruth

See also 5P.1.

5H.1   BERTMAN, STEPHEN. "Symmetrical Design in the Book of Ruth." Journal of Biblical Literature, 84 (1965), 165-168.
A new critical investigation of the unifying plan, or "architecture," of Ruth.

5H.2   CAMPBELL, EDWARD F., JR. "The Hebrew Short Story: A Study of Ruth," in A Light unto My Path: Old Testament Studies in Honor of Jacob M. Myers. Edited by Howard N. Bream, Ralph D. Heim, and Carey A. Moore. Philadelphia: Temple University Press, 1974, pp. 83-101.
Surveys scholarly criticism on Ruth and argues that the book is a highly creative literary masterpiece produced by a Hebrew "singer of tales," designed to combine "the joy and pathos of Israelite common life with the serious purpose of God."

5H.3   CAMPBELL, EDWARD F., JR. Ruth. The Anchor Bible, 7. Garden City, New York: Doubleday, 1975. 209 pp.
See 1A.1.

5H.4   CROOK, MARGARET B. "The Book of Ruth: A New Solution." Journal of Bible and Religion, 16 (1948), 155-160.
Speculation on the origins of the book.

5H.5   GORDIS, ROBERT. "Love, Marriage, and Business in the Book of Ruth: A Chapter in Hebrew Customary Law," in A Light unto My Path: Old Testament Studies in Honor of Jacob M. Myers. Edited by Howard N. Bream, Ralph D. Heim, and Carey A. Moore. Philadelphia: Temple University Press, 1974, pp. 241-264.
Important background on marriage and land customs that create confusion in the book of Ruth. Challenges the accepted view that Ruth illustrates a levirate marriage; rather, the transaction involves "a genuine example of the redemption of land, which had been sold under the stress of economic want to an outsider."

The Old Testament: Individual Books

5H   Ruth

5H.6   HALS, RONALD M. The Theology of the Book of Ruth. Facet
        Books Biblical Series, No. 23. Philadelphia: Fortress Press,
        1969. 93 pp.
            Theological background on references to God in Ruth, and a
        comparison of the book with the Court history of David, the
        Joseph story, Genesis 24, and Esther.

5H.7   KNIGHT, GEORGE A. F. Ruth and Jonah: The Gospel in the Old
        Testament. Torch Bible Commentaries. Revised edition. Lon-
        don: SCM Press, 1966. 93 pp.
            Introductions and passage-by-passage commentaries from a
        Christian perspective. The books are treated together because
        of their similar perspective on Jewish nationalism.
        Bibliographies.

5H.8   RAUBER, D[ONALD] F. "Literary Values in the Bible: The
        Book of Ruth." Journal of Biblical Literature, 89 (1970),
        27-37.
            A spirited defense of the literary approach to the Bible
        envelopes this close reading of Ruth. The story is not a sim-
        ple, delightful, idyll, but a carefully contrived work de-
        manding response to its deliberate patterns. Reprinted as
        "The Book of Ruth" in 3F.22, pp. 163-176.

5H.9   ROWLEY, H[AROLD] H. "The Marriage of Ruth." Harvard Theo-
        logical Review, 40 (1947), 77-99.
            Background on ancient Israelite marriage customs as they
        elucidate the story of Ruth. Reprinted in 4B.9, pp. 169-194.

5H.10   TRIBLE, PHYLLIS. "Two Women in a Man's World: A Reading of
        the Book of Ruth." Soundings, 54 (1976), 251-279.
            A detailed reading of the story, seeing it as a comedy in
        which women work out their own salvation, "for it is God who
        works in them."

5I   Samuel - Kings (Including Saul, David, Solomon, Elijah, Elisha)

See also 3A.4; 3F.21; 3J.15; 4A.12; 4E.10; 4F.2, 4; 4G.1; 5C.3; 5H.6.

5I.1   ARPALI, BOAZ. "Caution: A Biblical Story! Comments on the
        Story of David and Bathsheba and on the Problems of the Bibli-
        cal Narrative." Ha-Sifrut, 2 (1969-1971), 580-607 (Hebrew
        original), 686-684 (English summary).
            A response to 5I.7. Though this essay demonstrated multi-
        ple layers of irony in the David and Bathsheba story, it
        failed to point out the true moral purpose of this irony.

The Old Testament: Individual Books

5I.2   GROS LOUIS, KENNETH R. R. "The Difficulty of Ruling Well:
King David of Israel." Semeia, 8 (1977), 15-33.
Sees the narrative "patterned on the differences between
David in his private encounters and David in his public acti-
vities." See 3F.15.

5I.3   GROS LOUIS, KENNETH R. R. "Elijah and Elisha," in 3F.22,
pp. 177-190.
The two prophets stand out as misfits in their culture.
The writer of Kings has not only conveyed a theological message through them, but has also created in them two believable
and memorable literary characters.

5I.4   MCCARTHY, DENNIS J. "The Inauguration of Monarchy in Israel: A Form-Critical Study of 1 Samuel 8-12." Interpretation,
27 (1973), 401-412.
Studies the structure, genre, setting, and intention of the
passage.

5I.5   MCCARTHY, DENNIS J. "2 Samuel 7 and the Structure of the
Deuteronomic History." Journal of Biblical Literature, 84
(1965), 131-138.
This chapter, like other key passages noted by Noth, helps
tie the Deuteronomic history together.

5I.6   PERRY, MENAKHEM, and MEIR STERNBERG. "Caution: A Literary
Text! Problems in the Poetics and the Interpretation of Biblical Narrative." Ha-Sifrut, 2 (1969-1971), 608-663 (Hebrew
original), 682-679 (English summary).
A rebuttal of two rejoinders (5I.1 and 5I.10) to the authors' 5I.7. Answers these critics and defends a modern
literary approach to the Bible.

5I.7   PERRY, MENAKHEM and MEIR STERNBERG. "The King through
Ironic Eyes: The Narrator's Devices in the Biblical Story of
David and Bathsheba and Two Excursuses on the Theory of the
Narrative Text." Ha-Sifrut, 1 (1968), 263-292 (Hebrew original), 452-449 (English summary).
A reading of the David and Bathsheba story (2 Samuel 11)
emphasizing irony produced by a system of gaps in the text
which must be filled by the reader. Comments on the theory of
literary narration in general. See 5I.1, 10.

5I.8   PFEIFFER, ROBERT H., with WILLIAM G. POLLARD. The Hebrew
Iliad: The History of the Rise of Israel under Saul and David.
New York: Harper & Brothers, 1957. 154 pp.
An original translation of the Court histories of Saul and
David ("probably by the priest Ahimaaz") separated from the

5I   Samuel - Kings

later materials with which it now appears in the Bible. Presented as the Hebrew national epic. General and chapter introductions provide background. Appendixes include translations
of related biblical material.

5I.9   ROTH, WOLFGANG. "You Are the Man! Structural Interaction
in 2 Samuel 10-12." Semeia, 8 (1977), 1-13.
A structural analysis of the David and Bathsheba story in
terms of parable, myth, and polemic. See 3F.15.

5I.10   SIMON, URIEL. "An Ironic Approach to a Bible Story: On the
Interpretation of the Story of David and Bathsheba." Ha-
Sifrut, 2 (1969-1971), 598-607 (Hebrew original), 684-683
(English summary).
A response to 5I.7. This essays brings a "too modern"
literary approach to the biblical story of David and Bathsheba.

5I.11   WHYBRAY, R. N. The Succession Narrative: A Study of 2 Samuel 9-20; 1 Kings 1 and 2. Studies in Biblical Theology,
Second Series, No. 9. London: SCM Press, 1968. 128 pp.
Argues that the narrative, though primarily a political
document, has important literary overtones and can be considered a historical novel. Relates the narrative to the
Wisdom tradition (particularly to Proverbs and the Joseph
narrative) and to the political novel in ancient Egypt and
Israel.

5J   Chronicles - Ezra - Nehemiah

See also 4A.16.

5J.1   MYERS, JACOB M. Chronicles. Two volumes. The Anchor
Bible, 12-13. Garden City, New York: Doubleday, 1965. Volume
12, 333 pp.; volume 13, 304 pp.
See 1A.1 and 4C.7.

5J.2   MYERS, JACOB M. Ezra - Nehemiah. The Anchor Bible, 14.
Garden City, New York: Doubleday, 1965. 352 pp.
See 1A.1.

5K   Esther

See also 5H.6; 5P.1; 5X.1; 6F.4.

5K.1   MOORE, CAREY A. Esther. The Anchor Bible, 7B. Garden
City, New York: Doubleday, 1971. 190 pp.
See 1A.1.

5L   Job

See also 3D.10; 3F.1; 3L.8; 3M.7-8; 4B.1, 6, 10-11; 4C.23; 4E.7, 10,
21-22; 4G.5.

5L.1   BLAKE, WILLIAM. Blake's Job: William Blake's Illustrations
of the Book of Job. With an introduction and commentary by S.
Foster Damon. Providence, Rhode Island: Brown University
Press, 1966. 76 pp.
Each illustration accompanied by a brief analysis by the
editor. See 5L.8.

5L.2   COOK, ALBERT. The Root of the Thing: A Study of Job and
the Song of Songs. Bloomington: Indiana University Press,
1968. 174 pp.
A study of two books yoked together because they were both
written in dramatic form and both apparently struggled to at-
tain positions in the canon. Written by a classical scholar
known for his studies and translations of Greek literature.

5L.3   CROOK, MARGARET BRACKENBURY. The Cruel God: Job's Search
for the Meaning of Suffering. Boston: Beacon Press, 1959.
237 pp.
A reading of Job which attempts to use recent scholarly
discoveries to probe the meaning of the poem and the story of
how it came to be written. Appendixes include a short dis-
course on the form of Hebrew poetry. Selected bibliography.

5L.4   DAICHES, DAVID. "The Book of Job," in his More Literary
Essays. Edinburgh: Oliver & Boyd, 1968, pp. 268-274.
First published in Commentary (May 1966). A review of
5L.12, presenting some of Daiches' own observations on Job.

5L.5   DRIVER, SAMUEL ROLLES, and GEORGE BUCHANAN GRAY. A Critical and Exegetical Commentary on the Book of Job: Together
with a New Translation. Two volumes. The International Critical Commentary. New York: Charles Scribner's Sons, 1921.
Volume 1, 454 pp.; volume 2, 372 pp.
The translation and passage-by-passage commentary are accompanied by extensive introductory material and philological
notes. Part of the introduction is reprinted as "The Purpose
and Method of the Writer" in 5L.36.

5L.6   FINE, HILLEL A. "The Tradition of a Patient Job." Journal
of Biblical Literature, 74 (1955), 28-32.
Besides the prologue and epilogue, chapters 27 and 28 form
a unit showing us the patient, not the bitter, Job. Reprinted
in 5L.19, pp. 118-124.

5L   Job

5L.7   FREEDMAN, DAVID NOEL. "The Elihu Speeches in the Book of
         Job: A Hypothetical Episode in the Literary History of the
         Work." Harvard Theological Review, 61 (1968), 51-59.
              Observations on the origin and placing of the speeches
         (Job 32-37).

5L.8   FRYE, NORTHROP. "Blake's Reading of the Book of Job," in
         Spiritus Mundi: Essays on Literature, Myth, and Society.
         Bloomington: Indiana University Press, 1976, pp. 228-244.
              A revision of Frye's earlier essay in William Blake: Essays
         for S. Foster Damon (1969). An analysis of Blake's illustra-
         tions, which reveal the poet's "critical analysis of the book,
         of the whole Bible of which it forms a microcosm. . . ." See
         5L.1.

5L.9   GLATZER, NAHUM N., ed. The Dimensions of Job: A Study and
         Selected Readings. New York: Schocken Books, 1969. 320 pp.
              An introductory essay on various ways of interpreting Job
         and selected modern readings by different scholars, grouped
         according to kind of approach followed. Bibliography. See
         3E.10, 12; 5L.14, 25, 27, 29.

5L.10   GOOD, EDWIN M. "Job and the Literary Task: A Response."
         Soundings, 56 (1973), 470-484.
              A reply to David Robertson (5L.34), taking issue with some
         of what he says (especially his commission of the intentional
         fallacy), but ultimately praising his reading of the book as
         literature.

5L.11   GOODHEART, EUGENE. "Job and the Modern World." Judaism,
         10 (1961), 21-28.
              Modern sensibilities have sometimes clouded our under-
         standing of Job. Reprinted in 5L.36.

5L.12   GORDIS, ROBERT. The Book of God and Man: A Study of Job.
         Chicago: University of Chicago Press, 1965. 401 pp.
              An extensive commentary followed by the author's own trans-
         lation of Job. The reading of the poem "is derived largely
         from my recognition of its architectonic structure and its
         inner unity." Bibliography. See 5L.4.

5L.13   GORDIS, ROBERT. "The Conflict of Tradition and Experience:
         The Book of Job," in Great Moral Dilemmas in Literature, Past
         and Present. Edited by R. M. MacIver. Religion and Civiliza-
         tion Series. New York: Institute for Religious and Social
         Studies, 1956, pp. 155-178.
              A reading of Job emphasizing the conflict between his ex-
         perience and the Hebrew tradition that suffering is a retri-
         bution for sin.

5L.14   GORDIS, ROBERT. "The Temptation of Job--Tradition versus
         Experience in Religion." Judaism, 4 (1955), 195-208.
             A study of Job in light of the conflict between his personal
         experience and Hebrew tradition. An abridgement appears in
         5L.9, pp. 74-85.

5L.15   GROS LOUIS, KENNETH R. R. "The Book of Job," in 3F.22, pp.
         226-266.
             Two threads link this complex dialogue: a discussion of the
         problem of evil and suffering in a world controlled by an all-
         good God; and a shifting in Job's attitudes toward God: the
         debate with his friends leads Job to conclusions he otherwise
         might not have held.

5L.16   GUILLAUME, A. Studies in the Book of Job: With a New Trans-
         lation. Edited by John MacDonald. Supplement 2 to the Annual
         of Leeds University Oriental Society. Leiden: E. J. Brill,
         1968. 162 pp.
             An introduction, arguing that the book was written in Ara-
         bia and is the product of an Arabian milieu, is followed by a
         translation and translator's notes.

5L.17   HANSON, ANTHONY, and MIRIAM HANSON. The Book of Job: A Com-
         mentary. New York: Collier Books, 1962. 127 pp.
             Originally published as The Book of Job: Introduction and
         Commentary (1953). An introduction providing background is
         followed by a chapter-by-chapter commentary aimed at the
         general reader.

5L.18   HIRSH, NORMAN D. "The Architecture of the Book of Job."
         CCAR Journal, 16, no. 1 (January 1969), 32-35.
             Argues for the unity of the book. "The poet utilized older
         materials [adapting] them skillfully to his purposes."

5L.19   HONE, RALPH E., ed. The Voice out of the Whirlwind: The
         Book of Job. Materials for Analysis. San Francisco: Chandler
         Publishing Company, 1960. 343 pp.
             A resource anthology reprinting the King James Job, fol-
         lowed by introductions, sermons, essays, drawings, and poetry
         on Job and its modern dramatic adaptations. Bibliography.
         See 3E.12; 5L.6.

5L.20   HURVITZ, AVI. "The Date of the Prose Tale of Job Linguis-
         tically Reconsidered." Harvard Theological Review, 67 (1974),
         17-34.
             The language of Job 1-2 and 42:7-17 indicates a late, post-
         Exilic date.

5L   Job

5L.21   IRWIN, WILLIAM A. "Job and Prometheus." Journal of Religion, 30 (1950), 90-108.
         Compares the book of Job to Aeschylus' Prometheus Bound.

5L.22   IRWIN, WILLIAM A. "Job's Redeemer." Journal of Biblical
Literature, 81 (1962), 217-229.
         Examines the significance of the redeemer cited by Job in
the light of Near Eastern mythology.

5L.23   IRWIN, WILLIAM A. "Poetic Structure in the Dialogue of
Job." Journal of Near Eastern Studies, 5 (1946), 26-39.
         An advanced study of form emphasizing the high degree of
"symmetry and grace" in the poem.

5L.24   JUNG, CARL G. "Answer to Job," in The Portable Jung. Edited by Joseph Campbell. Translated by R. F. C. Hull. New
York: Viking Press, 1971, pp. 519-650.
         The famous psychoanalyst uses the story of Job as a means
of coming to terms with religious traditions and ideas from a
mythical and psychological perspective. Provides background
for a literary reading of the book. Available in several other
editions and translations.

5L.25   KALLEN, HORACE M. The Book of Job as a Greek Tragedy. New
York: Hill & Wang, 1959. 189 pp.
         Originally published in 1918. An essay arguing that Job
was originally a drama in the Euripidean tradition is followed
by a chapter on the Joban philosophy of life (reprinted in
5L.9, pp. 175-181), and a reconstruction of the text of Job
in dramatic form.

5L.26   MACKENZIE, R. A. F. "The Sufferings of Job." America, 136
(1977), 242.
         A brief note arguing that Job has been transformed by a
double experience: "unexplained suffering, followed by a new
understanding of God."

5L.27   MACLEISH, ARCHIBALD. "God Has Need for Man." Sermon delivered in Farmington, Connecticut, 1955. In 5L.9, pp. 278-
286.
         The poet's reading of the book argues that God must allow
Job to suffer because God has need of man and man's love.

5L.28   MILLER, WARD S. "Job and the New Criticism." Conference
on Christianity and Literature Newsletter, 19, no. 3 (1970),
26-31.
         Applies the methods of the new criticism to the Revised
Standard Version of Job. Studies the structure, techniques,

and poetic expression of the book and concludes "it comes out a thoroughly well-unified artistic whole."

5L.29   MURRAY, GILBERT.   "Aeschylus as a Poet of Ideas."   Chapter 3 of Aeschylus: The Creator of Tragedy. Oxford: Clarendon Press, 1940, pp. 87-110.
A discussion of the Greek playwright's speculative answers to "the question of Job," contrasting Job and Prometheus. Part reprinted as "Prometheus and Job" in 5L.36. Part reprinted as "Beyond Good and Evil" in 5L.9, pp. 194-197.

5L.30   POLZIN, ROBERT.   "The Framework of the Book of Job." Interpretation, 28 (1974), 182-200.
A structural analysis arguing that apparent inconsistencies in the book serve to point up the contradiction between traditional teaching about divine justice and personal experience. See 3L.4.

5L.31   POLZIN, ROBERT, and DAVID ROBERTSON, eds.   "Studies in the Book of Job." Semeia, 7 (1977).   160 pp.
Articles and replies by several scholars on readings of Job as comedy and drama. Contents: J. William Whedbee, "The Comedy of Job" (pp. 1-39; response by David Robertson, pp. 41-44); Luis Alonso-Schökel, "Toward a Dramatic Reading of the Book of Job" (pp. 45-61; response by James Crenshaw, pp. 63-69); John A. Miles, Jr., "Gagging on Job, or the Comedy of Religious Exhaustion" (pp. 71-126; response by Robert Polzin, pp. 127-133); James G. Williams "Comedy, Irony, Intercession: A Few Notes in Response" (pp. 135-145); William Urbrock, "Reconciliation of Opposites in the Dramatic Ordeal of Job" (pp. 147-154).

5L.32   POPE, MARVIN H.   Job.   Third edition.   The Anchor Bible, 15A. Garden City, New York: Doubleday, 1973. 501 pp.
See 1A.1 and 4C.7.

5L.33   REXROTH, KENNETH.   "Classics Revisited: XXVII, The Book of Job." Saturday Review of Literature (23 April 1966), p. 21.
A brief commentary on the themes of the book. Reprinted in 5L.36.

5L.34   ROBERTSON, DAVID.   "The Book of Job: A Literary Study." Soundings, 56 (1973), 446-469.
A study of the "aesthetic texture" of Job--especially its irony. The book shows that "while God may be more powerful than we are, he is beneath us on scales that measure love, justice, and wisdom. . . . From this fact we take our comfort." See 5L.10.

5L   Job

5L.35   SANDERS, PAUL S. "The Passion of Job," in <u>Masterpieces of</u>
<u>Western Literature: Contemporary Essays in Interpretation.</u>
Edited by Alex Page and Leon Barron. Dubuque, Iowa: William
C. Brown, 1966, volume 1, pp. 135-146.
  The central, personal question raised by Job is "Will God
hear when I cry unto him?" The book answers that God allows
himself to be experienced in the midst of human affairs.
Bibliography.

5L.36   SANDERS, PAUL S., ed. <u>Twentieth Century Interpretations of</u>
<u>the Book of Job.</u> Englewood Cliffs, New Jersey: Prentice-Hall,
1968. 125 pp.
  A collection of critical commentaries by various scholars.
Bibliography. <u>See</u> 3G.5; 4I.9; 5L.5, 11, 29, 33, 39.

5L.37   SARNA, NAHUM M. "Epic Substratum in the Prose of Job."
<u>Journal of Biblical Literature</u>, 76 (1957), 13-25.
  Argues that the prologue and epilogue of the book are derived from an ancient epic of Job. An advanced study.

5L.38   SARNA, NAHUM M. "The Mythological Background of Job 18."
<u>Journal of Biblical Literature</u>, 82 (1963), 315-318.
  An advanced note on allusions to Canaanite mythology in
this chapter.

5L.39   SEWALL, RICHARD B. "The Book of Job." Chapter 2 of his
<u>The Vision of Tragedy</u>. New Haven: Yale University Press,
1959, pp. 9-24.
  A literary interpretation emphasizing Job as tragic hero.
Reprinted in 5L.36.

5L.40   SHAPLEY, HARLOW, "Out of the Whirlwind." <u>American Scholar</u>,
35 (1966), 690-694.
  Informal reflections on Job as "science-touched poetry."
Notes the scientific inquiry behind many of God's questions
in chapter 38.

5L.41   SNAITH, NORMAN H. <u>The Book of Job: Its Origin and Purpose</u>.
Studies in Biblical Theology. Second Series, No. 11. Naperville, Illinois: Alec R. Allenson, 1968. 126 pp.
  Background on, and a reading of, Job. Assumes that the
book is substantially the work of one man and that its primary
concern is not suffering, but the problem of the transcendent
God and his relationship to men.

5L.42   SPIVACK, CHARLOTTE. "Job and Faust: The Eternal Wager."
<u>Centennial Review</u> (Michigan State University), 15 (1971), 53-
69.

Includes a reading of Job which sees the book depicting "the discovery of the devil in deity and man's subsequent elevation through this knowledge."

5L.43   STEVENSON, WILLIAM BARRON.   Critical Notes on the Hebrew Text of the Poem of Job.   Aberdeen, Scotland: Aberdeen University Press, 1951.   178 pp.
Advanced notes suggesting major differences between the original Hebrew book and the folktale which now frames it.   Prefaces to the notes on the sections of the speeches provide a brief analysis of the poem.   See 5L.44.

5L.44   STEVENSON, WILLIAM BARRON.   The Poem of Job: A Literary Study with a New Translation.   Schweich Lectures, 1943.   London: Oxford University Press, 1947.   131 pp.
Translates only the poetic passages of Job and argues that this "poem" should be studied separately.   Presents a reading of the poem emphasizing the poet's conception of Job's misfortunes and a more positive picture of the attitudes of Job's comforters.   Assesses the literary qualities and value of the poem and the nature of the traditions in which the poet worked.   See 5L.43.

5L.45   TERRIEN, SAMUEL.   Job: Poet of Existence.   Indianapolis: Bobbs-Merrill, 1957.   249 pp.
A reading of the poem, reprinting the King James Version section by section.   "Job is the poet of existence, because he sinks into the abyss only when he has tasted the fullness of creative concern."   Bibliography.

5L.46   ZHITLOWSKY, CHAIM.   "Job and Faust."   Translated, with an introduction by Percy Matenko, in Two Studies in Yiddish Culture.   Edited by Percy Matenko.   Leiden: E. J. Brill, 1968, pp. 71-162.
Originally published in 1919.   Identifies several analogies between these literary works.   "Their essential deep unison is their reference to the super-individual world of cultural creation in which the meaning of human life must be sought."

5M   Psalms

See also 1C.6; 3A.3-4; 4A.20; 4B.1, 11; 4C.23; 4G; 6D.7; 8E.2.

5M.1   BARTH, CHRISTOPH F.   Introduction to the Psalms.   Translated by R. A. Wilson.   New York: Charles Scribner's Sons, 1966.   87 pp.

5M   Psalms

A series of short articles providing background information
on different aspects of the Psalms. Bibliography.

5M.2   BIRKELAND, HARRIS.   The Evildoers in the Book of Psalms.
Oslo: Dybwad, 1955.   96 pp.
A study of Hebrew "enemies" depicted in the Psalms.

5M.3   BOLING, ROBERT G.   "'Synonymous' Parallelism in the Psalms."
Journal of Semitic Studies, 5 (1960), 221-255.
An advanced study of the metrical patterns of the Hebrew
psalter.

5M.4   CHASE, MARY ELLEN.   The Psalms for the Common Reader.   New
York: W. W. Norton, 1962.   208 pp.
Comments in everyday language on the nature and types of
psalms and on their literary characteristics. Bibliography.
See 5Q.4.

5M.5   CRAIGIE, P. C.   "The Comparison of Hebrew Poetry: Psalm 104
in the Light of Egyptian and Ugaritic Poetry."   Semitics, 4
(1974), 10-21.
Surveys previous comparative studies of the psalm and concludes that it is "distinctively Hebrew in . . . its praise of
Yahweh."

5M.6   CULLEY, ROBERT C.   Oral Formulaic Language in the Biblical
Psalms.   Near and Middle East Series, Vol. 4.   Toronto: University of Toronto Press, 1967.   145 pp.
Studies certain stylistic features in the Psalms in light
of what is known about oral style and composition. For the
more advanced reader. Bibliography.

5M.7   DAHOOD, MITCHELL,   Psalms.   Three volumes.   The Anchor
Bible, 16-17A.   Garden City, New York: Doubleday, 1966-1970.
See 1A.1. Volume 16 covers Psalms 1-50; volume 17, Psalms
51-100; volume 17A, Psalms 101-150 (also contains an appendix,
"The Grammar of the Psalter").

5M.8   DRIJVERS, PIUS.   The Psalms: Their Structure and Meaning.
New York: Herder and Herder, 1965.   281 pp.
A study by a Catholic theologian. Introductory chapters
cover the Psalms as prayer, the Psalms' origin, and the nature
of Hebrew poetry; later chapters deal with the various kinds
of psalms. Bibliography.

5M.9   FREEDMAN, DAVID NOEL.   "The Structure of Psalm 137," in
Near Eastern Studies in Honor of William Foxwell Albright.
Edited by Hans Goedicke. Baltimore: Johns Hopkins Press,
1971, pp. 187-205.

An advanced study of the psalm focusing on its stylistic
devices and metrical structure.

5M.10   FRETHEIM, TERENCE E.   "Psalm 132: A Form Critical Study."
Journal of Biblical Literature, 86 (1967), 289-300.
An advanced study of the form and content of the psalm.

5M.11   GUNKEL, HERMANN.   _The Psalms: A Form-Critical Introduction_.
Translated by Thomas M. Horner.   Facet Books Biblical Series,
No. 19.   Philadelphia: Fortress Press, 1967.   64 pp.
A selection from his _Die Religion in Geschichte und Gegen-_
wart.   Describes "the nature of Hebrew poetic composition, its
rhetoric . . ., its different literary genres, and the style
and structure which characterize each."   The classic form-
critical study (dating from the turn of the twentieth century)
on the original forms and functions of the Psalms in Israelite
ritual.   Bibliography.

5M.12   GUTHRIE, HARVEY H., JR.   _Israel's Sacred Songs: A Study of_
Dominant Themes.   New York: Seabury Press, 1966.   251 pp.
A theologian's study of the meaning, but not the structure
or form, of sacred Hebrew poetry in the Bible (primarily, but
not exclusively, the Psalms).   Bibliography.

5M.13   JAMES, FLEMING.   _Thirty Psalmists: A Study in Personalities_
of the Psalter as Seen against the Background of Gunkel's Type-
Study of the Psalms.   New York: G. P. Putnam's Sons, 1938.
277 pp.
An analysis of selected psalms in an attempt to infer the
personalities of their authors.   Bibliography.   See 4E.12.
*Reprinted: Seabury Press, 1965.

5M.14   JOHNSON, AUBREY R.   _Sacral Kingship in Ancient Israel_.
Second edition.   Cardiff: University of Wales Press, 1967.
181 pp.
A study of "two well-known groups of Psalms, (1) the hymns
which celebrate the Kingship of Yahweh, and (2) the so-called
royal Psalms."

5M.15   KELLY, SIDNEY.   "Psalm 46: A Study in Imagery."   _Journal of_
Biblical Literature, 89 (1970), 305-312.
An advanced study of the image of Zion as a central motif
in this poem.

5M.16   LEWIS, C. S.   _Reflections on the Psalms_.   London: Geoffrey
Bles, 1958.   151 pp.
A series of essays based on Lewis' reading of the Psalms.
"This is not a work of scholarship. . . .   I write for the un-
learned about things in which I am unlearned myself."

5M   Psalms

5M.17   MOWINCKEL, SIGMUND. The Psalms in Israel's Worship. Two
volumes. Translated by D. R. Ap-Thomas. Nashville: Abingdon,
1967. Volume 1, 268 pp.; volume 2, 311 pp.
          A study by a Norwegian biblical scholar, emphasizing the
psalms as a product of cult worship in ancient Israel.
Bibliography.

5M.18   OBERHOLZER, J. P. "What Is Man . . .?" in De Fructu Oris
Sui: Essays in Honor of Adrianus van Selms. Edited by I. H.
Eybers, et al. Pretoria Oriental Series, No. 9. Leiden: E.
J. Brill, 1971, pp. 145-151.
          Studies the view of man expressed in the Psalms. The Psal-
mist "cannot escape from being man and thus enjoying solidarity
with mankind as a whole."

5M.19   O'CALLAGHAN, ROGER T. "Echoes of Canaanite Literature in
the Psalms." Vetus Testamentum, 4 (1954), 164-176.
          An advanced study of allusions in the Psalms.

5M.20   RINGGREN, HELMER. The Faith of the Psalmists. Philadelphia: Fortress Press, 1963. 160 pp.
          Studies "the religious experience expressed in these poems."
Chapters on the themes and emotions manifested in the Psalms.

5M.21   ROBERTSON, DAVID. "Literary Criticism of the Bible: Psalm
90 and Shelley's 'Hymn to Intellectual Beauty.'" Semeia, 8
(1977), 35-50.
          Studies the psalm as an aesthetic object. See 3F.15. Re-
printed in 4E.22.

5M.22   SABOURIN, LEOPOLD. The Psalms: Their Origin and Meaning.
Two volumes. New York: Alba House, 1969. Volume 1, 275 pp.;
volume 2, 395 pp.
          An introduction to the Psalter and its poems by a Catholic
biblical scholar. Follows Gunkel's classification of the
Psalms according to their liturgical use (See 5M.11).
Bibliography.

5M.23   TERRIEN, SAMUEL. The Psalms and Their Meaning for Today.
Indianapolis: Bobbs-Merrill, 1952. 278 pp.
          Background on the origin of the Psalms followed by explica-
tions of most of them, grouped according to type. For the
layman. Bibliography.

5M.24   TSEVAT, MATITIAHU. A Study of the Language of the Biblical
Psalms. Journal of Biblical Literature Monograph Series, No.
9. Philadelphia: Society of Biblical Literature, 1955.
161 pp.

An advanced study of "the idiom of the psalms as against the whole of classical Hebrew." Considers language patterns in the book of Psalms and in "psalms" from other parts of the Hebrew Bible. Draws some conclusions about the history and origin of the Psalms.

5M.25   VAN DOREN, MARK, and MAURICE SAMUEL. The Book of Praise: Dialogues on the Psalms. Edited by Edith Samuel. New York: John Day Company, 1975. 285 pp.
Informal conversations (originally radio broadcasts) by two men of letters on the language and themes of the Psalms. See 4E.26.

5M.26   WEISER, ARTUR. The Psalms: A Commentary. Translated by Herbert Hartwell. The Old Testament Library. Philadelphia: Westminster Press, 1962. 841 pp.
An introduction, followed by extensive line-by-line commentaries on each psalm. Reprints each psalm in the Revised Standard Version. Bibliography.

5M.27   WESTERMANN, CLAUS. The Praise of God in the Psalms. Translated by Keith R. Crim. Richmond, Virginia: John Knox Press, 1965. 172 pp.
Surveys the traditional categories of psalms (cf. Gunkel, 5M.11) and traces the theme of the praise of God through them. Bibliography.

5M.28   WEVERS, JOHN W. "A Study in the Form Criticism of Individual Complaint Psalms." Vetus Testamentum, 6 (1956), 80-96.
Investigates the origin and development of psalms of individual complaint, shedding light on their structure.

5M.29   ZYL, A. H. VAN. "The Unity of Psalm 27," in De Fructu Oris Sui: Essays in Honor of Adrianus van Selms. Edited by I. E. Eybers, et al. Pretoria Oriental Series, No. 9. Leiden: E. J. Brill, 1971, pp. 233-251.
The psalm is unified; what has been thought its "first half" is simply a long address leading into the lament.

5N   Proverbs

See also 4B.10-11; 4G.5; 5I.11.

5N.1   MILLER, PATRICK D., JR. "Apotropaic Imagery in Proverbs 6:20-22." Journal of Near Eastern Studies, 29 (1970), 129-130.
Notes imagistic parallels between Proverbs 6:20-22 and Deuteronomy 6:7-8 and 11:18-20.

5N Proverbs

5N.2   SCOTT, R. B. Y. Proverbs - Ecclesiastes. The Anchor Bible,
        18. Garden City, New York: Doubleday, 1965. 311 pp.
        See 1A.1 and 4C.7.

50 Ecclesiastes

See also 1C.6; 3F.1; 4B.10; 4E.10, 13, 21; 5N.2; 5P.1; 5X.1.

50.1   DAHOOD, MITCHELL. "Three Parallel Pairs in Ecclesiastes
        10:18: A Reply to Professor Gordis." Jewish Quarterly Review,
        62 (1971), 84-87.
        An advanced note citing an indebtedness of Ecclesiastes to
        ancient Ugaritic literature.

50.2   GORDIS, ROBERT. Koheleth--the Man and His World: A Study
        of Ecclesiastes. Third edition. New York: Schocken Books,
        1968. 431 pp.
        Sixteen chapters on background are followed by the Hebrew
        text with a new translation, a commentary, and auxiliary
        material. Special emphasis on the unknown author of the book
        and his style. Bibliography.

50.3   GORDIS, ROBERT. "Qoheleth and Qumran--A Study of Style."
        Biblica, 41 (1960), 395-410.
        An advanced study arguing that Ecclesiastes is a product of
        Hebrew literature and not of the Qumran community.

50.4   GROS LOUIS, KENNETH R. R. "Ecclesiastes," in 3F.22,
        pp. 267-282.
        A study of the personality of the Preacher as a literary
        persona created by the author/narrator. "Ultimately, there is
        no pessimism here. There is bluntness and honesty, and pain-
        ful self-awareness."

50.5   WRIGHT, ADDISON G. "The Riddle of the Sphinx: The Struc-
        ture of the Book of Qoheleth." Catholic Biblical Quarterly,
        30 (1968), 313-334.
        When the structure of Ecclesiastes is recognized it reveals
        one central theme: "the impossibility of understanding what God
        has done."

5P Song of Songs

See also 3H.4; 4B.9; 4G.5; 5L.2.

5P.1   BETTAN, ISRAEL. The Five Scrolls: A Commentary on the Song
of Songs, Ruth, Lamentations, Ecclesiastes, Esther. The Jewish Commentary for Bible Readers. Cincinnati: Union of American Hebrew Congregations, 1950. 270 pp.
         A modern Jewish commentary.

5P.2   GORDIS, ROBERT. The Song of Songs: A Study, Modern Translation, and Commentary. Texts and Studies of the Jewish Theological Seminary of America, Vol. 20. New York: Jewish Theological Seminary of America, 1954. 122 pp.
         Surveys the history of the interpretation of the book and
argues that it is an anthology of Hebrew love poems spanning
five centuries. The commentary provides notes to the translation. Bibliography.

5P.3   GRAVES, ROBERT. The Song of Songs: Text and Commentary.
Illustrations by Hans Erni. New York: Clarkson N. Potter,
1973. Pages unnumbered.
         A translation of the book. An introduction discusses the
origin of the Song and its relation to other Near Eastern
literature.

5P.4   LANDSBERGER, FRANZ. "Poetic Units within the Song of
Songs." Journal of Biblical Literature, 73 (1954), 203-216.
         Sees the book as a collection of several poems containing
more units than are usually recognized.

5P.5   POPE, MARVIN H. Song of Songs. The Anchor Bible, 7C.
Garden City, New York: Doubleday, 1977. 767 pp.
         See 1A.1.

5Q   The Prophets: General Studies

See also 1B.19; 3A.3, 13; 3F.37; 4A.13; 4B.1; 4C.21; 4E.22; 4F.4;
5W.1.

5Q.1   AVNI, ABRAHAM. "Inspiration in Plato and the Hebrew Prophets." Comparative Literature, 20 (1968), 55-63.
         A comparison of Greek and Hebrew poetic theories as illus-
trated in Plato and the Prophets. Differences derive largely
from "the divergent Platonic and Hebrew notions of divinity."

5Q.2   BEWER, JULIUS A., ed. The Prophets in the King James Version, with Introduction and Critical Notes. New York: Harper
& Brothers, 1955. 671 pp.

5Q   The Prophets: General Studies

> Texts of the Prophetic books, in chronological order, are accompanied by extensive notes and introductions.

5Q.3   BLANK, SHELDON H.   "Irony by Way of Attribution."   Semitics, 1 (1970), 1-6.
A study of how the biblical prophets often attribute thoughts to others for ironic effect.

5Q.4   CHASE, MARY ELLEN.   The Prophets for the Common Reader. New York: W. W. Norton, 1963.   183 pp.
A companion to 5M.4, treating the six Classical Prophets: Amos, Hosea, Isaiah of Jerusalem, Micah, Jeremiah, Isaiah of Babylon.   Units on who were the Prophets, the Prophets as men, Hebrew prophecy as literature, and characteristic selections from the Prophets.   Selected bibliography.

5Q.5   HEATON, E. W.   The Old Testament Prophets.   Baltimore: Penguin Books, 1958.   187 pp.
A revision of his His Servants the Prophets (1949).   Background on the prophets and their times.   Bibliography.

5Q.6   HESCHEL, ABRAHAM J.   The Prophets.   Two volumes.   New York: Harper & Row, 1962.   Volume 1, 251 pp.; volume 2, 307 pp.
A study of the personalities of the prophets based on a reading of their words.   An important chapter on "Prophecy and Poetic Inspiration" includes a brief history of the study of the Bible as literature from Longinus on.

5Q.7   NAPIER, B. D.   Prophets in Perspective.   Nashville: Abingdon Press, 1963.   128 pp.
Background on prophetism and the prophetic movement, rather than on the individual prophets.

5Q.8   PORTEOUS, N. W.   "The Hebrew Prophets," in 3B.3, pp. 40-46.
A brief introduction to the prophets, for the layman.

5Q.9   ROBINSON, THEODORE H.   Prophecy and the Prophets in Ancient Israel.   Second edition.   London: Gerald Duckworth, 1963. 224 pp.
General surveys of prophecy are followed by individual treatments of the major prophets and prophetic movements. Studies the possibility of "any ecstatic element in the life of the canonical prophets."   Covers the part played by each prophet in the development of Israelite religion.

5Q.10   ROWLEY, H[AROLD] H., ed.   Studies in Old Testament Prophecy. Edinburgh: T & T Clark, 1950.   218 pp.

Essays by different individuals providing scholarly background on the prophets. Of special interest for the Bible as literature are W. F. Albright's "The Psalm of Habakkuk" (pp. 1-18) and A. R. Johnson's "Jonah 2:3-10: A Study in Cultic Phantasy" (pp. 82-102), on the "psalm of Jonah."

5Q.11   SCOTT, R. B. Y. The Relevance of the Prophets. Revised edition. New York: Macmillan, 1968.   248 pp.
A study of prophecy and the prophets emphasizing their importance for today. See 4B.10.

5Q.12   VAWTER, BRUCE. The Conscience of Israel: Pre-Exilic Prophets and Prophecy. New York: Sheed & Ward, 1961.   318 pp.
Theological background from a Roman Catholic perspective. Covers the nature and development of prophecy and the Hebrew prophets of the seventh and eighth centuries B.C.

5Q.13   WESTERMANN, CLAUS. Basic Forms of Prophetic Speech. Translated by Hugh Clayton White. Philadelphia: Westminster Press, 1967.   222 pp.
A form-critical study focusing on judgment speeches in the Prophets. Surveys the recent history of research and the nature of the subject, and investigates judgment speeches directed at individuals and at Israel.

5Q.14   WILLIAMS, JAMES G. "Irony and Lament: Clues to Prophetic Consciousness." Semeia, 8 (1977), 51-74.
Studies the ironic poetry of the prophets (especially Amos, Isaiah, and Micah) who are "caught" between God and people. See 3F.15.

5R   The Prophets: Isaiah

See also 3A.4; 4A.20; 4B.6; 4E.10; 4H.2; 4I.1; 5Q.

5R.1   GROS LOUIS, KENNETH R. R. "Isaiah: Chapters 40-55," in 3F.22, pp. 208-225.
These chapters constitute a unified whole; they celebrate the rebirth and renewal surrounding an army returning triumphant from war.

5R.2   MCKENZIE, JOHN L. Second Isaiah. The Anchor Bible, 20. Garden City, New York: Doubleday, 1968.   301 pp.
See 1A.1.

5R.3   PAYNE, D. F. "Characteristic Word-Play in 'Second Isaiah': A Reappraisal." Journal of Semitic Studies, 12 (1967), 207-229.

5S   The Prophets: Jeremiah

      An advanced study criticizing the theory that Second Isaiah was fond of deliberate puns and double entendres.

5S   The Prophets: Jeremiah

See also 3A.4; 4B.6; 5Q; 6F.4.

  5S.1   BRIGHT, JOHN. "The Book of Jeremiah: Its Structure, Its Problems, and Their Significance for the Interpreter." *Interpretation*, 9 (1955), 259-278.
      An attempt "to describe the arrangement and literary form of the book, to discuss the manner of its composition, and to suggest how these things have a bearing upon the solution of its critical problems. . . ."

  5S.2   BRIGHT, JOHN. *Jeremiah*. The Anchor Bible, 21. Garden City, New York: Doubleday, 1965. 514 pp.
      See 1A.1 and 4C.7.

  5S.3   HOLLADAY, WILLIAM L. *The Architecture of Jeremiah 1-20*. Lewisburg, Pennsylvania: Bucknell University Press, 1976. 204 pp.
      Applies rhetorical criticism to study the structure of the first part of the book. Notes how literary units are joined by associations of sounds, key words, phrases, or ideas. Studies a series of cycles that compose this part of the book. Bibliography.

  5S.4   HOLLADAY, WILLIAM L. "Jeremiah and Moses: Further Observations." *Journal of Biblical Literature*, 85 (1966), 17-27.
      Jeremiah saw himself as the "prophet like Moses" (Deuteronomy 18:18). Focuses on "parallels between Jeremianic poetry and the Song of Moses (Deuteronomy 32), and the meaning of Jeremiah 15:16."

  5S.5   HOLLADAY, WILLIAM L. "Prototype and Copies: A New Approach to the Poetry-Prose Problem in the Book of Jeremiah." *Journal of Biblical Literature*, 79 (1960), 351-367.
      A study of the stylistic connections between the poetic and prose sections of the book.

  5S.6   HOLLADAY, WILLIAM L. "The Recovery of Poetic Passages of Jeremiah." *Journal of Biblical Literature*, 85 (1966), 401-435.
      An advanced study attempting to refine our understanding of what is poetry and what is prose in the book.

5S.7   HOLLADAY, WILLIAM L. "Style, Irony, and Authenticity in Jeremiah." Journal of Biblical Literature, 81 (1962), 44-54.
A study of the prophet's style as a means of determining what parts of the book actually record his words.

5T Lamentations

See also 4G.5; 5P.1.

5T.1   HILLERS, DELBERT R. Lamentations. The Anchor Bible, 7A. Garden City, New York: Doubleday, 1972. 164 pp.
See 1A.1.

5U The Prophets: Ezekiel

See also 4E.9; 4H.2; 5Q.

5U.1   BROWNLEE, WILLIAM H. "Ezekiel's Poetic Indictment of the Shepherds." Harvard Theological Review, 51 (1958), 191-203.
An advanced commentary on the poetic nature of Ezekiel 34:1-10.

5U.2   DEVRIES, SIMON J. "Remembrance in Ezekiel: A Study of an Old Testament Theme." Interpretation, 16 (1962), 58-64.
"It is the purpose of this article to show briefly what Ezekiel had to say about remembrance, and to place this in relation to his view of Israel's destiny."

5U.3   MCKENZIE, JOHN L. "Mythological Allusions in Ezekiel 28: 12-18." Journal of Biblical Literature, 75 (1956), 322-327.
Mythological references in this passage allude to the Hebrew tradition of Paradise in Genesis 2-3 and not to foreign myths.

5V Daniel

See also 4B.9; 4H; 5X.1; 6F.4.

5V.1   HARTMAN, LOUIS F., and ALEXANDER A. DILELLA. The Book of Daniel. The Anchor Bible, 23. Garden City, New York: Doubleday, 1978. 360 pp.
See 1A.1.

5W The Minor Prophets

5W. The Minor Prophets (Except Jonah)

See also 4H.2; 5Q.

5W.1   HARPER, WILLIAM RAINEY. A Critical and Exegetical Commen-
         tary on Amos and Hosea. The International Critical Commentary,
         Vol. 23. New York: Charles Scribner's Sons, 1905. 610 pp.
            A 186 page introduction (providing background on the pre-
         prophetic movement as well as on Amos and Hosea) is followed
         by a line-by-line commentary. An older study, still consi-
         dered valuable.

5W.2   MAYS, JAMES L. "Words about the Words of Amos: Recent
         Study of the Book of Amos." Interpretation, 13 (1959), 259-
         272.
            A survey of commentary on Amos.

5W.3   SUPER, A. S. "Figures of Comparison in the Book of Amos."
         Semitics, 3 (1973), 67-80.
            Studies some of the metaphors, similes, and images in the
         book.

5W.4   WATTS, JOHN D. W. "An Old Hymn Preserved in the Book of
         Amos." Journal of Near Eastern Studies, 15 (1956), 33-39.
            Analyzes three hymnic portions of Amos: 4:13, 5:8, and
         9:5-6. An advanced study.

5X Jonah

See also 4E.10; 4I.5; 5H.8; 5Q.10.

5X.1   BICKERMAN, ELIAS. Four Strange Books of the Bible: Jonah,
         Daniel, Koheleth, and Esther. New York: Schocken Books, 1967.
         247 pp.
            Comments by a classical scholar interested in biblical
         books written under Greek intellectual influence. Studies
         these books "as witnesses to the mentality of men of that
         period in the ancient Near East."

5X.2   "Jonah: A Special Supplement." Response, 8, no. 2 (Summer
         1974), 7-26.
            Contains a new translation of the book, an essay on its
         language by Everett Fox, and Joel Rosenberg's "Jonah and the
         Prophetic Vocation," which comments on the book's meaning
         within the rabbinic tradition.

5X.3   LANDES, GEORGE M. "The Kerygma of the Book of Jonah: The
Contextual Interpretation of the Jonah Psalm." Interpretation,
21 (1967), 3-31.
          Argues that the psalm (Jonah 2:2-9) fits appropriately with
the prose passages of the book.

5X.4   MORE, JOSEPH. "The Prophet Jonah: The Story of an Intra-
psychic Process." American Imago, 27 (1970), 3-11.
          A reading of the book in the light of modern psychodynamic
theory.

5X.5   RAUBER, D. F. "Jonah--The Prophet as Schlemiel." The
Bible Today, 49 (1970), 29-38.
          Discusses the need to read the Bible as literature, and
then reads Jonah as a comic work with characteristic Jewish
intellectual humor. "Jonah himself illustrates the theme of
'reason gone mad,' while the Lord represents 'reason made
mischievous.'"

5X.6   WARSHAW, THAYER S. "The Book of Jonah," in 3F.22, pp. 191-
207.
          A reading of the book emphasizing two "lessons": that love
is more important than justice, and that it should be universal rather than restricted to one group.

6 The Apocrypha

6A The Apocrypha: Historical and Cultural Background

See also 2C; 2D; 2E.12; 2I.3; 3B; 4A; 7A; 7D.6.

6A.1   HENGEL, MARTIN. Judaism and Hellenism: Studies in Their
        Encounter in Palestine during the Early Hellenistic Period.
        Translated by John Bowden. Two volumes. London: SCM Press,
        1974. Volume 1, 326 pp.; volume 2, 337 pp.
            Social, religious, and historical background for the Apoc-
        rypha and New Testament. Bibliography.

6A.2   PFEIFFER, ROBERT H. History of New Testament Times with an
        Introduction to the Apocrypha. New York: Harper & Brothers,
        1949. 573 pp.
            Historical background on Judaism from 200 B.C. to A.D. 200,
        followed by introductions to the individual books of the Apoc-
        rypha. Bibliography.

6A.3   TARN, W. W. Hellenistic Civilization. Third edition. Re-
        vised by the author and G. T. Griffith. London: Edward Arnold,
        1952. 382 pp.
            Historical and cultural background on Greek civilization
        from 323 B.C. to 30 B.C. Includes a chapter on "Hellenism and
        the Jews" (pp. 210-238).

6B The Apocrypha: Scholarly and Theological Background

See also 2C; 2E.13; 2I.4; 3C; 6F.1.

6B.1   CHARLES, R. H. Religious Development between the Old and
        the New Testaments. London: Williams & Norgate, 1914. 256 pp.
            An older study providing theological and literary back-
        ground to the Old Testament Apocrypha and Pseudepigrapha.

6C The Apocrypha: Introductions and Commentaries

See also 2H; 4C.8, 29-30; 6A.2; 7C.2.

The Apocrypha

₁C Introductions and Commentaries

6C.1   DENTAN, ROBERT C. The Apocrypha, Bridge of the Testaments:
        A Reader's Guide to the Apocryphal Books of the Old Testament.
        Greenwich, Connecticut: Seabury Press, 1954. 128 pp.
            An introduction to the Apocrypha and its literature for the
        general reader. Bibliography.

6C.2   GOODSPEED, EDGAR J. The Story of the Apocrypha. Chicago:
        University of Chicago Press, 1939. 160 pp.
            Background on the Apocrypha and each of its books.
        Bibliography.

6C.3   MEECHAM, H. G. "The Apocrypha," in 3B.3, pp. 52-57.
            A brief introduction to the literary forms in the Apocrypha.

6C.4   METZGER, BRUCE M. An Introduction to the Apocrypha. New
        York: Oxford University Press, 1957. 286 pp.
            Introductions to each book are sandwiched between chapters
        providing general background. Bibliography.

6C.5   SCHÜRER, EMIL. The Literature of the Jewish People in the
        Time of Jesus. Edited by Nahum N. Glatzer. New York:
        Schocken Books, 1972. 430 pp.
            Part of a classic nineteenth-century work, The Jewish Peo-
        ple in the Time of Jesus Christ. (See 7A.20.) Brief commen-
        taries on the Apocrypha and other Jewish literature of the
        era. Bibliography on the Apocrypha, 1900-1970.

6D The Literary Milieu of the Apocrypha (Including the Dead
    Sea Scrolls)

See also 1D.43; 3F.1; 4C.8; 50.3; 6C.5; 7D; 8F.4.

6D.1   BURROWS, MILLAR. The Dead Sea Scrolls. New York: Viking
        Press, 1955. 459 pp.
            Discusses the nature and significance of the Scrolls and
        provides translations of several manuscripts. Index is pub-
        lished in 6D.2. Illustrations and bibliography.

6D.2   BURROWS, MILLAR. More Light on the Dead Sea Scrolls: New
        Scrolls and New Interpretations, with Translations of Impor-
        tant Recent Discoveries. New York: Viking Press, 1958. 453
        pp.
            A sequel to 6D.1. Covers implications of the Scroll mate-
        rial for biblical study and other aspects of the Judeo-
        Christian background. Includes an index to the earlier volume.
        Bibliography.

The Apocrypha

6D.3   CROSS, FRANK MOORE, JR.   The Ancient Library of Qumran and
Modern Biblical Studies.   Revised edition.   Garden City, New
York: Doubleday, 1961.   280 pp.
   Background on the Dead Sea Scrolls and their significance
for Old Testament study.

6D.4   DAVIES, A POWELL.   The Meaning of the Dead Sea Scrolls.
New York: New American Library, 1956.   144 pp.
   A survey for the general reader covering the background and
nature of the Scrolls and their relation to the Bible.

6D.5   GASTER, THEODORE H.   The Dead Sea Scriptures in English
Translation.   Revised edition.   Garden City, New York: Doubleday, 1964.   430 pp.
   A translation for laymen with introduction and notes.   Ren-
derings of biblical passages are not included.

6D.6   MILIK, J. T.   Ten Years of Discovery in the Wilderness of
Judaea.   Translated by J. Strugnell.   Studies in Biblical
Theology, No. 26.   London: SCM Press, 1959.   176 pp.
   Background on the Dead Sea Scrolls.   The story of their
discovery and information about the Scrolls and the people who
produced them.   Illustrations and bibliography.

6D.7   SANDERS, J. A.   The Dead Sea Psalms Scroll.   Ithaca, New
York: Cornell University Press, 1967.   186 pp.
   A translation of this Scroll with an introduction and com-
mentary on the apocryphal psalms it contains.   Bibliography.

6D.8   STENDAHL, KRISTER, ed.   The Scrolls and the New Testament.
London: SCM Press, 1958.   320 pp.
   An anthology of articles by different scholars giving background on new perspectives on the New Testament provided by
the Dead Sea Scrolls.

6D.9   VERMES, G.   The Dead Sea Scrolls in English.   Baltimore:
Penguin Books, 1962.   255 pp.
   Background on the Scrolls followed by translations of some
of the documents, including a selection of biblical interpretations.   Bibliography.

6D.10   WILSON, EDMUND.   The Dead Sea Scrolls 1947-1969.   London:
W. H. Allen, 1969.   320 pp.
   Revised and expanded version of The Scrolls from the Dead
Sea (1955).   A literary critic presents background on the his-
tory and significance of the Scrolls and reports on his two
journeys to Palestine to seek out information about them.

The Apocrypha

6D   The Literary Milieu

6D.11   WOODWARD, KENNETH L., and JOSEPH B. CUMMING, JR.   "Books
          the Bible Left Out."   _Newsweek_, 90 (28 November 1977), 121-126.
          An account of a recent attempt to compile and translate in-
          to English large portions of biblical pseudepigrapha written
          between 200 B.C. and A.D. 200.   The project, directed by James
          H. Charlesworth of Duke University, should be completed in
          1980.

6E   The Apocrypha as Literature: General Studies

See 3F; 4E.2; 4E.25; 7E.1.

6F   The Apocrypha as Literature: Individual Books

See also 4B.11; 4E.26; 4F.2.

6F.1   BATTISTONE, JOSEPH JOHN.   "An Examination of the Literary
          and Theological Background of the Wisdom Passage in the Book
          of Baruch."   Dissertation, Duke University, 1968.   Abstracted
          in _Dissertation Abstracts_, 29 (1968), 4543A.
          Studies questions of authorship, date, themes, and concepts.
          More biblical scholarship than literary analysis.

6F.2   CRAVEN, TONI.   "Artistry and Faith in the Book of Judith."
          Semeia, 8 (1977), 75-101.
          Studies literary parallels between the two parts of the
          book.   _See_ 3F.15.

6F.3   GOLDSTEIN, JONATHON A.   _1 Maccabees_.   The Anchor Bible, 41.
          Garden City, New York: Doubleday, 1976.   617 pp.
          See 1A.1.

6F.4   MOORE, CAREY A.   _Daniel, Esther, and Jeremiah: The Addi-
          tions_.   The Anchor Bible, 44.   Garden City, New York: Double-
          day, 1977.   404 pp.
          See 1A.1.

6F.5   MYERS, JACOB M.   _1 and 2 Esdras_.   The Anchor Bible, 42.
          Garden City, New York: Doubleday, 1974.   408 pp.
          See 1A.1.

7 The New Testament as a Whole

7A The New Testament: Historical and Cultural Background

See also 2C; 2D; 2E.12; 2I.3; 3B; 6A; 7B.1; 7D.3-4; 7D.7; 8B.

7A.1   BOUQUET, A. C. Everyday Life in New Testament Times. New
        York: Charles Scribner's Sons, 1953. 256 pp.
        An illustrated survey of many aspects of ordinary life in
        Jesus' time. See the companion volume on the Old Testament
        (4A.7).

7A.2   BRÉHIER, EMILE. The Hellenistic and Roman Age. Translated
        by Wade Baskin. The History of Philosophy, Vol. 2. Chicago:
        University of Chicago Press, 1965. 261 pp.
        Helpful background on the intellectual milieu of the New
        Testament. Especially pertinent is chapter 8, "Hellenism and
        Christianity" (pp. 218-250). Bibliography.

7A.3   BULTMANN, RUDOLF. Primitive Christianity in its Contempo-
        rary Setting. Translated by R. H. Fuller. New York: World
        Publishing Company, 1956. 240 pp.
        Examines the philosophy of life in primitive Christianity
        by considering the "new" religion in terms of its Hebrew and
        Hellenistic heritage. Provides a cultural background for New
        Testament literature. Bibliography.

7A.4   DAUBE, DAVID. The New Testament and Rabbinic Judaism. The
        Jewish People: History, Religion, Literature. New York: Arno
        Press, 1973. 478 pp.
        An advanced study of the relationship between the New Tes-
        tament and traditional Judaism.

7A.5   DAVIES, W. D. Torah in the Messianic Age and/or the Age
        to Come. Journal of Biblical Literature Monograph Series,
        Vol. 7. Philadelphia: Society of Biblical Literature, 1952.
        107 pp.
        A scholarly monograph on the interaction between Judaism
        and early Christianity, providing background on the New
        Testament.

The New Testament as a Whole

7A Historical & Cultural Background

7A.6   DEWITT, NORMAN WENTWORTH. Epicurus and His Philosophy.
Minneapolis: University of Minnesota Press, 1954. 392 pp.
    Provides intellectual background to the New Testament. In-
cludes brief discussion of "Epicureanism in the New Testament."
Bibliography.

7A.7   DOLAN, JOHN P. Catholicism: An Historical Survey. Woodbury, New York: Barron's Educational Series, 1968. 256 pp.
    Background on the history and teachings of a major compo-
nent of Western Christianity. Chapter 1, "Catholicism in the
Hellenistic World," provides historical background on the New
Testament era. Bibliography.

7A.8   FARMER, WILLIAM REUBEN. Maccabees, Zealots, and Josephus:
An Inquiry into Jewish Nationalism in the Greco-Roman Period.
New York: Columbia University Press, 1956. 253 pp.
    Historical background for the New Testament. Bibliography.
See 7D.3.

7A.9   GLATZER, NAHUM N. Hillel the Elder: The Emergence of Classical Judaism. Revised edition. New York: Schocken Books,
1966. 90 pp.
    The story of Hillel (a Jewish contemporary of Herod the
Great), his teaching, and his era. Important cultural background for the New Testament. Bibliography.

7A.10   GRANT, FREDERICK C. Ancient Judaism and the New Testament.
New York: Macmillan, 1959. 173 pp.
    Places the New Testament in the context of its Jewish
heritage.

7A.11   GRANT, FREDERICK C. Roman Hellenism and the New Testament.
Edinburgh: Oliver & Boyd, 1962. 228 pp.
    Places the New Testament in the context of its historical
milieu. Bibliography.

7A.12   GRANT, R. M. Gnosticism and Early Christianity. Second
edition. New York: Columbia University Press, 1966. 251 pp.
    Background on the theological milieu of the later New Testa-
ment and New Testament Apocrypha. Bibliography.

7A.13   GUIGNEBERT, CHARLES. The Jewish World in the Time of Jesus.
New York: University Books, 1959. 302 pp.
    Translation of a work originally published in French in
1935. Historical and cultural background for the New Testament. Argues that Jesus must be viewed in the context of his
time: sectarian syncretistic Judaism of the first century.

The New Testament as a Whole

7A.14   JEREMIAS, JOACHIM. Jerusalem in the Time of Jesus: An Investigation into Economic and Social Conditions during the New
Testament Period. Translated by F. H. and C. H. Cave. Philadelphia: Fortress Press, 1969. 421 pp.
Background and context for the New Testament.

7A.15   JONAS, HANS. The Gnostic Religion: The Message of the Alien
God and the Beginnings of Christianity. Second edition. Bos-
ton: Beacon Press, 1963. 378 pp.
Theological and historical background for the New Testament.
Bibliography.

7A.16   KLAUSNER, JOSEPH. The Messianic Idea in Israel: From Its
Beginning to the Completion of the Mishnah. Translated by
W. F. Stinespring. London: George Allen & Unwin, 1956. 559
pp.
Background on the development of the Messianic idea from
the time of the prophets through c. A.D. 200. Written by a
Jew for Jewish readers; includes an appendix on "The Jewish
and the Christian Messiah." Third part of a trilogy which includes 8B.6 and 8I.9.

7A.17   MOWINCKEL, S. He That Cometh. Translated by G. W. Ander-
son. New York: Abingdon Press, n.d. 542 pp.
Background on the concept of the Messiah in Judaism.
Bibliography.

7A.18   PEROWNE, STEWART. The Life and Times of Herod the Great.
London: Hodder & Stoughton, 1956. 186 pp.
A biography of the infamous king of Judea, providing back-
ground for the Gospels.

7A.19   REICKE, BO. The New Testament Era: The World of the Bible
from 500 B.C. to A.D. 100. Translated by David E. Green.
Philadelphia: Fortress Press, 1968. 351 pp.
Historical background for the New Testament and the Apocrypha. Bibliography.

7A.20   SCHÜRER, EMIL. The History of the Jewish People in the Age
of Jesus Christ (175 B.C.--A.D. 135). Revised and translated
by Geza Vermes and Fergus Millar. Edinburgh: T & T Clark,
1973. 632 pp.
A revision of the first volume of a classic nineteenth-
century work, The Jewish People in the Time of Jesus Christ,
presenting the political history of the period. See 6C.5.

The New Testament as a Whole

7A Historical & Cultural Background

7A.21   SHERWIN-WHITE, A. N. Roman Society and Roman Law in the New Testament. The Sarum Lectures, 1960-1961. Oxford: Clarendon Press, 1963. 216 pp.
Legal, administrative, and municipal background for Acts and the synoptic Gospels.

7B The New Testament: Scholarly and Theological Background

See also 1D.41; 2C; 2E.13; 2I.4; 3C; 6D.8; 7C; 7I.1, 3; 8A; 8B.1, 4, 7, 9; 8E.6-7; 8F.3, 5; 8I.7.

7B.1   BRAATEN, CARL E. History and Hermeneutics. New Directions in Theology Today, Vol. 2. Philadelphia: Westminster Press, 1966. 205 pp.
An advanced study providing background on the relationship between a historical and a more conservative view of New Testament events.

7B.2   BULTMANN, RUDOLF. Theology of the New Testament. Translated by Kendrick Grobel. Two volumes. New York: Charles Scribner's Sons, 1951-1955. Volume 1, 376 pp.; volume 2, 284 pp.
The work of a major theologian, providing important background. Bibliography. Available in a single volume: *New York: Charles Scribner's Sons, 1970.

7B.3   CULLMAN, OSCAR. Immortality of the Soul or Resurrection of the Dead: The Witness of the New Testament. London: Epworth Press, 1958. 60 pp.
Argues that the New Testament concept of resurrection is often erroneously associated with the Greek belief in the immortality of the soul. Contrasts the literary depictions of the deaths of Jesus and Socrates. Reprinted in Immortality and Resurrection. Edited by Krister Stendahl. New York: Macmillan, 1965.

7B.4   DAVIES, W. D. The Gospel and the Land: Early Christianity and Jewish Territorial Doctrine. Berkeley: University of California Press, 1974. 537 pp.
A study of "the motif and problem of the land . . . for the understanding of the emergence of Christianity." Bibliography.

7B.5   DODD, C. H. The Apostolic Preaching and Its Developments: Three Lectures, with an Appendix on Eschatology and History. New York: Harper & Row, 1964. 96 pp.
Theological background focusing on the central narrative pattern in the New Testament.

128

7B.6   DODD, C. H. <u>New Testament Studies</u>. Manchester, England: Manchester University Press, 1953. 190 pp.
   Eight essays providing background. Includes three essays on the preliterary traditions behind the Gospels ("The Framework of the Gospel Narrative," "A New Gospel," "Matthew and Paul"), and two more on "The Mind of Paul." Reprinted with minor corrections: *1966.

7B.7   MONTGOMERY, ROBERT M., and W. RICHARD STEGNER. <u>Kerygma</u>. Auxiliary Studies in the Bible. Nashville: Abingdon Press, 1970.
   A programmed learning text for college students, treating "kerygma," or early Christian preaching in the New Testament.

7C   The New Testament: Introductions and Commentaries

<u>See also</u> 2H; 7E.

7C.1   BARNETT, ALBERT E. <u>The New Testament: Its Making and Meaning</u>. Revised edition. Nashville: Abingdon Press, 1958. 304 pp.
   Commentaries on each book in chronological order. Bibliography.

7C.2   CORNFELD, GAALYAHU, ed. <u>Daniel to Paul: Jews in Conflict with Graeco-Roman Civilization</u>. New York: Macmillan, 1962. 389 pp.
   Background for the general reader prepared by Israeli scholars. Covers the Apocrypha, the New Testament, and other lesser-known writings. Illustrations. Companion to 4C.6.

7C.3   DAVIES, W. D. <u>Invitation to the New Testament: A Guide to Its Main Witnesses</u>. An Anchor Book. Garden City, New York: Doubleday, 1969. 552 pp.
   An attempt to introduce "the central thrust of the foundation document of Christianity" to lay readers by describing and explaining the major documents of the New Testament.

7C.4   FULLER, REGINALD H. <u>A Critical Introduction to the New Testament</u>. Studies in Theology. Second edition. London: Gerald Duckworth, 1971. 221 pp.
   A companion to 4C.2, replacing an earlier volume with the same title by A. S. Peake (1919). Discusses New Testament books in order of composition.

7C.5   GRANT, ROBERT M. <u>A Historical Introduction to the New Testament</u>. New York: Harper & Row, 1963. 448 pp.

7C Introductions and Commentaries

A discussion of New Testament literature, history, and theology. Literary analysis focuses on "the author's purposes and achievements by means of a detailed examination of the works themselves."

7C.6   HARVEY, A. E. The New English Bible Companion to the New Testament. Oxford: Oxford University Press, 1970. 858 pp.
A verse-by-verse commentary on the books of this New Testament.

7C.7   HENSHAW, T. New Testament Literature in the Light of Modern Scholarship. London: George Allen & Unwin, 1952. 454 pp.
Introductory chapters on New Testament background are followed by accounts of the "authorship, recipients, date and place of composition, sources, purpose, contents, characteristics, and historical value" of each New Testament book. Bibliography.

7C.8   HOSKYNS, SIR EDWYN, and NOEL DAVY. The Riddle of the New Testament. Third edition. London: Faber & Faber, 1947. 238 pp.
A historical investigation of "the relation between Jesus of Nazareth and the Primitive Christian Church." Studies the language and text, as well as other dimensions, of the New Testament. Bibliography.

7C.9   HUNTER, ARCHIBALD M. Interpreting the New Testament: 1900-1950. Philadelphia: Westminster Press, 1951. 144 pp.
A survey of New Testament studies in the first half of the twentieth century for the general reader.

7C.10   KEE, HOWARD CLARK, FRANKLIN W. YOUNG, and KARLFRIED FROEH-LICH. Understanding the New Testament. Third edition. Englewood Cliffs, New Jersey: Prentice-Hall, 1973. 461 pp.
"We have sought to set forth the story of Christian origins against the background of its own social, political, and cultural setting. . . ." Illustrations. Companion to 4C.1.

7C.11   KÜMMEL, WERNER GEORG. Introduction to the New Testament. Revised edition. Translated by Howard Clark Kee. Nashville: Abingdon Press, 1975. 629 pp.
This standard introduction provides extensive background on the origin of the New Testament writings and canon and the history of the text. Includes observations about the literary character of each New Testament book. Bibliography.

7C.12   LOISY, ALFRED. The Origins of the New Testament. Translated by L. P. Jacks. London: George Allen & Unwin, 1950. 332 pp.

An advanced historical analysis of the origins and early developments of the New Testament books. Also published in one volume with his The Birth of the Christian Religion (New Hyde Park, New York: University Books, 1962).

7C.13   MCNEILE, A. H. An Introduction to the Study of the New Testament. Second edition. Revised by C. S. C. Williams. Oxford: Clarendon Press, 1953. 494 pp.
An introduction to the history and contents of the New Testament.

7C.14   MARXSEN, W. Introduction to the New Testament: An Approach to Its Problems. Translated by G. Buswell. Philadelphia: Fortress Press, 1968. 298 pp.
A shorter introduction providing background for the beginner.

7C.15   NEILL, STEPHEN. The Interpretation of the New Testament 1861-1961. New York: Oxford University Press, 1964. 368 pp.
A survey of the history of interpretation over the period designed for the layman.

7C.16   The Pelican New Testament Commentaries. Baltimore: Penguin Books.
A series of volumes presenting contemporary scholarship to the layman. Each volume contains the text of a New Testament book or books accompanied by paragraph-by-paragraph commentary. Volumes include: The Gospel of St. Mark (D. E. Nineham, ed., 1963); The Gospel of St. Matthew (John Fenton, ed., 1963); The Gospel of St. Luke (G. B. Caird, ed., 1963); The Gospel of St. John (John Marsh, ed., 1968); Paul's Letters from Prison (J. L. Houlden, ed., 1970); Paul's First Letter to Corinth (John Ruef, ed., 1971).

7C.17   PERRIN, NORMAN. The New Testament: Proclamation and Parenesis, Myth and History: An Introduction. New York: Harcourt Brace Jovanovich, 1974. 397 pp.
A general introduction, incorporating modern scholarship, designed for the "secular" student rather than the religious apologist. Bibliography.

7C.18   PRICE, JAMES L. Interpreting the New Testament. Second edition. New York: Holt, Rinehart & Winston, 1971. 640 pp.
Background on each New Testament writing emphasizing historical criticism. Includes an outline and analysis of each book. Illustrations and bibliography.

The New Testament as a Whole

7C   Introductions and Commentaries

7C.19   SANDMEL, SAMUEL. A Jewish Understanding of the New Testa-
          ment. Cincinnati: Hebrew Union College Press, 1957. 353 pp.
          An introduction to the New Testament for Jewish readers.

7D   The Literary Milieu of the New Testament

See also 3F.26; chap. 6; 7C.2; 7E.2; 8A.13-14; 8H.2.

7D.1   BARRETT, C. K. The New Testament Background: Selected Docu-
          ments. London: SPCK, 1961. 300 pp.
          Selected texts from various areas of the New Testament
          world, translated and arranged to provide insight into the
          milieu of the Bible.

7D.2   GAER, JOSEPH. The Lore of the New Testament. Boston: Lit-
          tle, Brown, 1952. 383 pp.
          A collection of legends and folklore narratives relating to
          New Testament events, from the lineage of Jesus to stories
          about his Apostles and followers. Bibliography. See 4D.6.

7D.3   JOSEPHUS, FLAVIUS. Flavius Josephus: Selections from His
          Works. Edited by Abraham Wasserstein. The B'nai B'rith
          Jewish Heritage Classics. New York: Viking Press, 1974.
          318 pp.
          Selections from the writings of the famous first-century
          Jewish historian, providing primary historical and cultural
          background for the New Testament. Bibliography.

7D.4   JOSEPHUS, FLAVIUS. The Jewish War. Translated by G. A.
          Williamson. Baltimore: Penguin Books, 1977. 422 pp.
          The story of the Jewish uprising against the Romans in A.D.
          66, written by a Jewish leader (and Roman sympathizer) of the
          times. Important primary historical document providing New
          Testament background. Maps and bibliography. See 7A.8.

7D.5   HENNECKE, EDGAR. New Testament Apocrypha. Edited by Wil-
          helm Schneemelcher. Translated by R. McL. Wilson. Two vol-
          umes. Philadelphia: Westminster Press, 1963-1965. Volume 1,
          531 pp.; volume 2, 852 pp.
          Translations of apocryphal material are augmented by exten-
          sive introductions and notes.

7D.6   JAMES, MONTAGUE RHODES, editor and translator. The Apocry-
          phal New Testament. Oxford: Clarendon Press, 1953. 625 pp.
          New translations of many apocryphal New Testament books and
          summaries of others. Brief introductions to each.
          Bibliography.

7D.7   KEE, HOWARD CLARK. The Origins of Christianity: Sources
         and Documents. Englewood Cliffs, New Jersey: Prentice-Hall,
         1973. 284 pp.
            Translations of nonbiblical historical and literary docu-
         ments from the first and second centuries before and after
         Christ. Primary sources for historical, literary, and cultu-
         ral background of the New Testament.

7D.8   The Lost Books of the Bible and the Forgotten Books of Eden.
         New York: New American Library, 1974. 562 pp.
            The Lost Books of the Bible (first published in 1926) con-
         tains apocryphal New Testament books such as Nicodemus, Her-
         mas, and The Lost Gospel of Peter. The Forgotten Books of
         Eden (1927) contains Old Testament pseudepigraphal material
         such as The Psalms of Solomon, The Secrets of Enoch, and books
         attributed to each of the twelve sons of Jacob. The present
         volume reprints this noncanonical material, in translation.

7E The New Testament as Literature: General Studies

See also 1B.18; 3E.3; 3F; 7C.11.

7E.1   ASIMOV, ISAAC. Asimov's Guide to the Bible. Volume 2: The
         New Testament. New York: Equinox Books (Avon), 1969. 637 pp.
            A companion to 4E.3, covering selected books from the Apoc-
         rypha as well as all books of the New Testament. Maps.

7E.2   BARNETT, ALBERT E. Paul Becomes a Literary Influence. Chi-
         cago: University of Chicago Press, 1941. 291 pp.
            An advanced study showing the influence of Paul's letters
         on other New Testament writers and other early Christian
         authors. Uses the Greek text.

7E.3   BEARDSLEE, WILLIAM A. Literary Criticism of the New Testa-
         ment. Guides to Biblical Scholarship, New Testament Series.
         Philadelphia: Fortress Press, 1970. 96 pp.
            Chapters on literary aspects of various parts of the New
         Testament. Deals with "literary criticism" of the Bible in
         both its older sense--the search for sources--and its newer
         sense--the application of the principles of the criticism of
         fiction and poetry to the study of biblical narratives. Anno-
         tated bibliography.

7E.4   CLARKE, M. L. Rhetoric at Rome: A Historical Survey. Re-
         printed with corrections. London: Cohen & West, 1966.
         210 pp., passim.

7E   General Studies

Background on style in the New Testament era. Chapter 14, "Rhetoric and Christianity," briefly treats biblical literary style.

7E.5   JONSSON, JAKOB. Humour and Irony in the New Testament: Illuminated by Parallels in Talmud and Midrash. Reykjavik: Bokautgafa Menningarsjods, 1965. 299 pp.
An attempt to get closer to the historical picture of Jesus and his contemporaries by examining the possibility of humor and irony in the canonical writings by and about them. Bibliography.

7E.6   JUEL, DONALD, with JAMES S. ACKERMAN and THAYER S. WARSHAW. An Introduction to New Testament Literature. Nashville: Abingdon Press, 1978. 368 pp.
Designed primarily for students and teachers of literature, providing background on and analyses of the New Testament as literature. Focus on the Gospels and Acts, with one chapter each on Paul's letters and Revelation. Annotated bibliography.

7E.7   PATTERSON, CHARLES H. The New Testament: Notes. Lincoln, Nebraska: Cliffs Notes, 1965. 101 pp.
Summaries and brief commentaries on the books. Bibliography.

7E.8   PETERSEN, NORMAN R. Literary Criticism for New Testament Critics. Guides to Biblical Scholarship, New Testament Series. Philadelphia: Fortress Press, 1978. 92 pp.
Argues for a literary analysis of the Bible that will complement the historical-critical approach. Discusses literary problems in the historical-critical paradigm and proposes a literary-critical model for historical criticism. Presents case studies of Mark (story time and plotted time in the narrative) and Luke-Acts (narrative world and real world).

7E.9   POWYS, JOHN COOPER. "The Bible as Literature: The New Testament," in his Enjoyment of Literature. New York: Simon & Schuster, 1938, pp. 35-52.
Romantic reflections on the value of the New Testament as literature focusing mainly on Luke's Gospel. "What St. Luke's Jesus did was to crack the heavy stone rolled by the privileged and the powerful and the clever and the scientific upon the spirit of man."

7E.10   PRITCHARD, JOHN PAUL. A Literary Approach to the New Testament. Norman, Oklahoma: University of Oklahoma Press, 1972. 366 pp.

A systematic literary look at each section of the New Testament. Assumes rhetoric and poetics to be within the realm of literature, and argues that "the Gospels, the Acts, and the Apocalpyse are artistic creations designed to persuade"-- though attention is paid to the Epistles, too. Glossary of literary and biblical terms. Bibliography.

7E.11   RHEIN, FRANCIS BAYARD. Barron's Simplified Approach to the New Testament. Woodbury, New York: Barron's Educational Series, 1968. 155 pp.
An outline for the nonspecialist. Background material, and detailed analyses and summaries of each book. A shorter treatment of much the same material found in 7E.12. Bibliography.

7E.12   RHEIN, FRANCIS BAYARD. Understanding the New Testament. Revised edition. Woodbury, New York: Barron's Educational Series, 1974. 402 pp.
Formerly published as An Analytical Approach to the New Testament (1966). An "introductory text for students of history, literature, or religion." Includes extensive background information and summaries and analyses of each book. Maps. Bibliography. See 3D.9; 7E.11.

7E.13   SCOTT, ERNEST FINDLAY. The Literature of the New Testament. Records of Civilization Sources and Studies, Vol. 14. New York: Columbia University Press, 1932. 325 pp.
A complement to Julius Bewer's work on the Old Testament (4E.4), which was originally part of this series. Some attention to the aesthetic nature of the New Testament. But "what we seek from it almost to the exclusion of all else, is a first-hand knowledge of the origin and nature of the Christian religion." Bibliography.

7E.14   SPIVEY, ROBERT A., and D. MOODY SMITH, JR. Anatomy of the New Testament: A Guide to Its Structure and Meaning. London: Macmillan, 1969. 528 pp.
A college text designed as an introduction to the reading of the New Testament. Focus on the text more than on background, date, authorship, etc. Maps, illustrations, and bibliography.

7E.15   TRAWICK, BUCKNER B. The Bible as Literature: The New Testament. College Outline Series, No. 57. Second edition. New York: Barnes & Noble, 1968. 183 pp.
An introductory chapter on New Testament backgrounds is followed by an outline of, and brief commentary on, each New Testament book. Written by a professor of English. Bibliography. See 3D.9; 4E.25.

The New Testament as a Whole

7E General Studies

7E.16   VIOLI, UNICIO J. Review Notes and Study Guide to the New
Testament. New York: Monarch Press, 1964. 171 pp.
     Introductory chapters on historical and textual background,
followed by summaries and commentaries on the individual books.
Bibliography.

7F The New Testament as Literature: Narrative

See 3G; 7B.5-6; 7E.7; 7I.4; 7J.1; 8C.5, 7, 15; 8D.8; 8E.1, 11; 8J.10.

7G The New Testament as Literature: Poetry and Poetics

See also 3F.17; 3H; 7E.10; 7I.4; 8F.7; 8I.2; 8J.4.

7G.1   FILSON, FLOYD V. "How Much of the New Testament is Poetry?"
Journal of Biblical Literature, 67 (1948), 125-134.
     Much of what is sometimes called poetry in the New Testa-
ment is not poetry at all.

7H The New Testament as Literature: Myth and Legend

See also 3J; 7D.2; 7I.4; 8A.4; 8I.17.

7H.1   FAWCETT, THOMAS. Hebrew Myth and Christian Gospel. London:
SCM Press, 1973. 335 pp.
     A study of mythical elements in the New Testament.

7H.2   JONES, GERAINT VAUGHAN. Christology and Myth in the New
Testament: An Inquiry into the Character, Extent, and Interpretation of the Mythological Element in New Testament Christology. New York: Harper & Brothers, 1956. 295 pp.
     A response to Bultmann's "demythologizing." "My purpose is
rather to enquire how far New Testament concepts are
mythological. . . ."

7H.3   TOLKIEN, J. R. R. "On Fairy Stories," in his Tree and Leaf.
Boston: Houghton Mifflin, 1965, pp. 3-84.
     Provides background on myth and fairy tales by considering
the definition, origin, and uses of the latter. The epilogue
argues briefly that "the Gospels contain a fairy story, or a
story of a larger kind which embraces all the essence of
fairy-stories." See 3G.9. Originally published in *Essays
Presented to Charles Williams (Oxford University Press, 1947).

7I   The New Testament as Literature: Language and Linguistics

See also 3K; 7C.8; 7J; 8D.7.

7I.1   FUNK, ROBERT W. Language, Hermeneutic, and Word of God:
The Problem of Language in the New Testament and Contemporary
Theology. New York: Harper & Row, 1966. 335 pp.
A study of the role of language in the work of twentieth-
century theologians coupled with a study of two New Testament
literary forms--the parable and the letter--as products of
language. See 8C.16.

7I.2   TANNEHILL, ROBERT C. The Sword of His Mouth. Semeia Supplements, No. 1. Philadelphia: Fortress Press, 1975. 234 pp.
A study of selected sayings in the synoptic Gospels as
literature. Focuses on "the forceful and imaginative language"
of these sayings as opposed to their content alone.
Bibliography.

7I.3   VAN BUREN, PAUL M. The Secular Meaning of the Gospel:
Based on an Analysis of Its Language. New York: Macmillan,
1963. 223 pp.
Discussion of modern Christianity and secularism based on a
linguistic analysis of the Gospels. Does not comment on each
Gospel separately, but attempts to tie together a study of
theology and language.

7I.4   WILDER, AMOS N. Early Christian Rhetoric: The Language of
the Gospel. Cambridge, Massachusetts: Harvard University
Press, 1971. 167 pp.
An earlier edition (1964) was called The Language of the
Gospel. The introduction (xi-xxx) surveys the history of the
Bible as literature and defends a modern posture that sees
literary and theological approaches intertwined. Chapters
focus on New Testament language in terms of modes and genres,
dialogues, story, parable, poem, image, symbol, and myth. See
8C.16.

7J   The New Testament as Literature: Structuralism

See also 3K-L; 8C.5-7, 9, 14-15; 8D.2; 8I.19.

7J.1   CALLOUD, JEAN. Structural Analysis of Narrative. Translated by Daniel Patte. Semeia Supplements, No. 4. Philadelphia:
Fortress Press, 1976. 123 pp.
An introduction to the structuralist approach focusing on
the temptation of Jesus in the wilderness.

7J   Structuralism

7J.2   JOHNSON, ALFRED M., JR., ed. The New Testament and Structuralism: A Collection of Essays by Corina Galland, Claude
Chabral, Guy Vuillod, Louis Marin, and Edgar Haulotte. Pittsburgh Theological Monograph Series, No. 11. Pittsburgh:
Pickwick Press, 1976. 347 pp.
          An anthology for advanced students of this field. Most of
the articles originally appeared in the French journal Langa-
ges (June 1971). In addition to essays covering general aspects of the field, there are specific structuralist analyses
of the women at the tomb, Jesus before Pilate (both by Marin),
and the "Text" of the Passion (by Chabral). Bibliography.

7J.3   VIA, DAN O., JR. Kerygma and Comedy in the New Testament:
A Structuralist Approach to Hermeneutic. Philadelphia: Fortress Press, 1975. 191 pp.
          A description/justification for "a structuralist-literary
approach to New Testament hermeneutic," followed by analyses
of the writings of Paul and Mark's Gospel. Argues that death
and resurrection--which loom large in Paul and Mark--lie at
the origins of Greek comedy and that certain motifs which
emerged as comedy developed also appear in these biblical
texts.

8 The New Testament: Individual Books

8A   The Gospels: General Studies

See also 3F.26; 7A.18, 21; 7B.6; 7E.6; 7H.3; 7I.2-4.

8A.1   BEARE, FRANCIS WRIGHT. The Earliest Records of Jesus. New
        York: Abingdon Press, 1962. 254 pp.
            Notes on the text of the synoptic Gospels are "not . . . a
        commentary . . ., [but are designed] to lead the student into
        an understanding of the nature of the materials with which he
        has to deal, and of the motives and methods of the Evange-
        lists." Bibliography.

8A.2   BULTMANN, RUDOLF. Form Criticism: Two Essays on New Testa-
        ment Research. Translated by Frederick C. Grant. New York:
        Harper & Row, 1962. 171 pp.
            Contains "The Study of the Synoptic Gospels" by Bultmann
        and "Primitive Christianity in the Light of Gospel Research"
        by Karl Kundsin. Provides background on the study of the oral
        traditions behind the written Gospels.

8A.3   BULTMANN, RUDOLF. The History of the Synoptic Tradition.
        Translated by John Marsh. New York: Harper & Row, 1963.
        460 pp.
            An advanced form-critical study of the Gospels tracing
        their preliterary history.

8A.4   DIBELIUS, MARTIN. From Tradition to Gospel. Translated by
        Bertram Lee Woolf. New York: Charles Scribner's Sons, n.d.
        317 pp.
            A study of form criticism or the investigation of oral tra-
        ditions behind the Gospels. Includes treatment of literary
        types such as legends and myths as they relate to the New
        Testament.

8A.5   FARMER, WILLIAM R. The Synoptic Problem: A Critical Analy-
        sis. Dillsboro, North Carolina: Western North Carolina Press,
        1976. 320 pp.

8A The Gospels: General Studies

> Background on the history and nature of the scholarly ques-
> tion about the origins of the synoptic Gospels and their rela-
> tionship to each other. Advanced.

8A.6   HADAS, MOSES, and MORTON SMITH. <u>Heroes and Gods: Spiritual</u>
<u>Biographies in Antiquity</u>. Religious Perspectives, Vol. 13.
New York: Harper & Row, 1965. 280 pp.
A study of the aretalogy, an ancient literary genre presenting a "formal account of the remarkable career of an impressive
teacher that was used as a basis for moral instruction." Includes a summary of Luke's Gospel designed to show to what extent the Gospel is related to this genre.

8A.7   KEE, HOWARD C. "Aretalogy and Gospel." <u>Journal of Bibli-</u>
<u>cal Literature</u>, 92 (1973), 402-422.
Argues that the genre "gospel" is not derived from an ancient literary form known as aretalogy. Mark's Gospel had no
literary precedent.

8A.8   KNOX, WILFRED L. <u>The Sources of the Synoptic Gospels</u>. Edited by H. Chadwick. Two volumes. Cambridge: Cambridge University Press, 1953-1957. Volume 1, 176 pp.; volume 2, 180 pp.
Source background for the first three Gospels.

8A.9   KOESTER, HELMUT H. "One Jesus and Four Primitive Gospels."
<u>Harvard Theological Review</u>, 61 (1968), 203-247.
Investigates the literary form of the gospel. "For this
type of literature, there are no pre- nor extra-Christian
parallels. . . ."

8A.10   MONTGOMERY, ROBERT M. <u>The Two-Source Theory and the Synop-</u>
<u>tic Gospels</u>. Auxiliary Studies in the Bible. Nashville:
Abingdon Press, 1970. 64 pp.
A programmed learning text for college students, dealing
with the evidence for this theory.

8A.11   MONTGOMERY, ROBERT M. and W. RICHARD STEGNER. <u>Forms in the</u>
<u>Gospels 1: The Pronouncement Stories</u>. Auxiliary Studies in
the Bible. Nashville: Abingdon Press, 1970. 72 pp.
A programmed text for college students dealing with form
analysis of the New Testament.

8A.12   TAYLOR, VINCENT. <u>The Formation of the Gospel Tradition</u>.
Second edition. London: Macmillan, 1949. 229 pp.
Background on the development of the traditions until they
emerged as full written gospels.

8A.13   THROCKMORTON, BURTON H., JR.   Gospel Parallels: A Synopsis of the First Three Gospels. Third edition, revised.   Nashville: Thomas Nelson & Sons, 1967.   217 pp.
  The synoptic Gospels printed in parallel columns for comparison.   Based on the Revised Standard Version.   Includes references to noncanonical gospels.

8A.14   VOTAW, CLYDE WEBER.   The Gospels and Contemporary Biographies in the Greco-Roman World.   Facet Books Biblical Series, No. 27.   Philadelphia: Fortress Press, 1970.   72 pp.
  Argues that there are parallels to the form of the canonical gospels in ancient biographies of figures like Socrates, Epictetus, and Apollonius of Tyana.   Bibliography.

8B   The Gospels: Jesus

See also 3J.16; 4G.6; 7B.3; 7C.8; 7E.5; 7J.1-2.

 8B.1   BORNKAMM, GÜNTHER.   Jesus of Nazareth.   Translated by Irene and Fraser McLuskey, with James M. Robinson.   New York: Harper & Row, 1960.   239 pp.
  A scholarly historical study of Jesus, his world, and his teachings.   Background for a literary perspective on the Gospels.

 8B.2   GUIGNEBERT, CHARLES.   Jesus.   Translated by S. H. Hooke. New York: University Books, 1956.   576 pp.
  An attempt to study the life and teachings of Jesus from historical record.   Background for the Gospels.   Bibliography.

 8B.3   HIGHET, GILBERT.   [Jesus as Teacher.]   In The Art of Teaching.   New York: Alfred A. Knopf, 1950, pp. 190-199.
  Characterizes Jesus by discussing his chief teaching methods as they can be deduced from the Gospels.

 8B.4   HUNTER, A. M.   The Work and Words of Jesus.   London: SCM Press, 1950.   196 pp.
  A brief life of Jesus.   Includes texts of the gospel sources Q, M, and L.

 8B.5   KEE, HOWARD CLARK.   Jesus in History: An Approach to the Study of the Gospels.   Second edition.   New York: Harcourt Brace Jovanovich, 1977.   320 pp.
  A study of Jesus' role in history as it was perceived by various segments of the early church, based on both biblical and extrabiblical sources.   Attempts to explain "the social

8B   The Gospels: Jesus

and cultural assumptions of the writers and their respective
communities."

8B.6   KLAUSNER, JOSEPH. Jesus of Nazareth: His Life, Times, and
Teaching. Translated by Herbert Danby. New York: Macmillan,
1959. 434 pp.
     An attempt to approach Jesus and his times historically,
written by a modern Jew for Jewish readers. First part of a
trilogy which includes 7A.16 and 8I.9.

8B.7   MCARTHUR, HARVEY K. The Quest through the Centuries: The
Search for the Historical Jesus. Philadelphia: Fortress Press,
1966. 195 pp.
     Background on the history of the scholarly quest to learn
about the historical Jesus from its earliest phases to the
mid-twentieth century.

8B.8   MUGGERIDGE, MALCOLM. Jesus: The Man Who Lives. New York:
Harper & Row, 1975. 191 pp.
     A personal reading of the gospel story of Jesus by a devout
Christian. Background for a literary reading of the Gospels.
Illustrations.

8B.9   SCHWEITZER, ALBERT. The Quest of the Historical Jesus: A
Critical Study of Its Progress from Reimarus to Wrede. Introduction by James M. Robinson. New York: Macmillan, 1968.
446 pp.
     The classic study of the attempts to seek out the histori-
cal personage, from the eighteenth century to the writing of
the book (1906).

8C   The Gospels: The Parables

See also 3I.2; 7I.1, 4; 8E.5.

8C.1   ARMSTRONG, EDWARD A. The Gospel Parables. New York: Sheed
& Ward, 1967. 219 pp.
     Backgrounds and interpretations from a Christian perspec-
tive. Over sixty parables are discussed individually.

8C.2   BAILEY, KENNETH EWING. Poet and Peasant: A Literary Cultural Approach to the Parables in Luke. Grand Rapids, Michigan: Wm. B. Eerdmans, 1976. 238 pp.
     Studies selected Lucan parables in terms of cultural milieu
and literary structure. Bibliography.

8C.3   BROWN, RAYMOND E.   "Parable and Allegory Reconsidered."
Novum Testamentum, 5 (1962), 36-45.
An allegorical reading of the parables is not as unjusti-
fied as scholars have thought.   Reprinted in his New Testament
Essays.   Milwaukee: Bruce Publishing Company, 1965, pp. 254-
264.

8C.4   CAVE, C. H.   "The Parables and the Scriptures."   New Testament Studies, 11 (1964/1965), 374-387.
The parables must be read in their "original context" of a
sermon based on the Scriptures.

8C.5   CROSSAN, JOHN DOMINIC, ed.   "The Good Samaritan."   Semeia,
2 (1974).   201 pp.
Special issue with structuralist analyses of this and other
parables.   Contents: Daniel Patte, "An Analysis of Narrative
Structure and the Good Samaritan" (pp. 1-26); Georges Crespy,
"The Parable of the Good Samaritan: An Essay in Structural
Research" (pp. 27-50); Robert W. Funk, "Structure in the Narrative Parables of Jesus" (pp. 51-73); "The Good Samaritan as
Metaphor" (pp. 74-81); John Dominic Crossan, "The Good Samaritan: Towards a Generic Definition of Parable" (pp. 82-112);
Critical Discussion (pp. 113-133); Amos N. Wilder, "The Parable of the Sower: Naivete and Method in Interpretation" (pp.
134-151); and William G. Doty, "The Parables of Jesus, Kafka,
Borges, and Others, with Structural Observations" (pp. 152-
193).

8C.6   CROSSAN, JOHN DOMINIC.   In Parables: The Challenge of the
Historical Jesus.   New York: Harper & Row, 1973.   159 pp.
A commentary on the parables, acknowledging their literary
nature.   Emphasizes a structuralist approach.   Bibliography.

8C.7   CROSSAN, JOHN DOMINIC, ed.   "Polyvalent Narration."   Semeia,
9 (1977).   153 pp.
Essays by different scholars present three different readings of the parable of the Prodigal Son: Mary Ann Tolbert,
"The Prodigal Son: An Essay in Literary Criticism from a Psy-
choanalytic Perspective" (pp. 1-20); Dan O. Via, "The Prodigal
Son: A Jungian Reading" (pp. 21-44); Bernard Scott, "The Prodigal Son: A Structuralist Interpretation" (pp. 45-74); and two
analyses of why it is possible for different readers to have
divergent interpretations of the same text: Susan Wittig, "A
Theory of Multiple Meanings" (pp. 75-104); and John Dominic
Crossan, "A Metamodel for Polyvalent Narration" (pp. 105-147).

8C.8   DODD, C. H.   The Parables of the Kingdom.   Revised edition.
New York: Charles Scribner's Sons, 1961.   190 pp.

8C   The Gospels: The Parables

An inquiry into the original intentions of the parables in
their historical settings.

8C.9   FUNK, ROBERT W., ed. "A Structuralist Approach to the
Parables." Semeia, 1 (1974). 286 pp.
Special issue with essays and replies by several critics on
this theme. Includes "A Basic Bibliography for Parables Re-
search" (pp. 236-274). Other contents: John Dominic Crossan,
"The Servant Parables of Jesus" (pp. 17-62), "Parable and
Example in the Teaching of Jesus" (pp. 63-104), "Structuralist
Analysis and the Parables of Jesus" (pp. 192-221); Dan O. Via,
Jr., "Parable and Example Story: A Literary-Structuralist Ap-
proach" (pp. 105-133), "A Response to Crossan, Funk, and
Petersen" (pp. 222-235); Norman R. Petersen, "On the Notion
of Genre in Via" (pp. 134-181); Robert W. Funk, "Critical
Note" (pp. 182-191).

8C.10   HUNTER, ARCHIBALD M. Interpreting the Parables. Philadelphia: Westminster Press, 1960. 126 pp.
Sketches the history of interpretation from apostolic times
and surveys modern interpretations of some sixty parables.
For the general reader.

8C.11   JEREMIAS, JOACHIM. The Parables of Jesus. Translated by
S. H. Hooke. The New Testament Library. Revised edition.
London: SCM Press, 1963. 248 pp.
An attempt to get back to "the earliest attainable form of
Jesus' parabolic teaching" followed by an analysis of the
parables' message. An adaptation for the general reader is
available: *Clarke, Frank. Rediscovering the Parables. New
York: Charles Scribner's Sons, 1966. See 8C.16.

8C.12   JONES, GERAINT VAUGHAN. The Art and Truth of the Parables:
A Study in Their Literary Form and Modern Interpretation.
London: SPCK, 1964. 262 pp.
A study of the parable as an art form. Sections on "The
Parables in Modern Interpretation," "The Parables as a Lite-
rary Form," and "The Parables and Human Existence." Select
bibliography.

8C.13   LINNEMANN, ETA. Jesus of the Parables: Introduction and
Exposition. Translated by John Sturdy. New York: Harper &
Row, 1966. 234 pp.
A discussion of the basic principles of parable interpretation is followed by expositions of selected parables. Bibliography. Published in Britain as Parables of Jesus: Introduction and Exposition. See 8C.16.

8C.14   PATTE, DANIEL, ed. Semiology and Parables: Exploration of
the Possibilities Offered by Structuralism for Exegesis.
Pittsburgh Theological Monograph Series, No. 9.   Pittsburgh:
Pickwick Press, 1976.   404 pp.
   Papers of the conference "Semiology and Exegesis" at Vander-
bilt University, May 1975.   Structuralist readings and respon-
ses by other critics on the interpretation of parables.   Con-
tents include: Dan O. Via, "The Parable of the Unjust Judge:
A Metaphor of the Unrealized Self" (pp. 1-32); Daniel Patte,
"Structural Analysis of the Parable of the Prodigal Son:
Toward a Method" (pp. 71-150); Walburga von Raffler Engel and
David Robertson, "The Semiotic Endeavor: Two Responses" (pp.
179-188); John Dominic Crossan, "Parable, Allegory, and Paradox" (pp. 247-281); and Susan Wittig, "Meaning and Modes of
Signification: Toward a Semiotic of the Parable" (pp. 319-347).

8C.15   PATTE, DANIEL.   "Structural Network in Narrative: The Good
Samaritan."   Soundings, 58 (1975), 221-242.
   Explains some basic principles of structural analysis and
applies them to a detailed study of the parable of the Good
Samaritan.   Reprinted in 3L.10.

8C.16   PERRIN, NORMAN.   "The Parables of Jesus as Parables, as
Metaphors, and as Aesthetic Objects: A Review Article."
Journal of Religion, 47 (1967), 340-346.
   Reviews of 7I.1, 4; and 8C.11, 13, 17.

8C.17   VIA, DAN OTTO, JR.   The Parables: Their Literary and Exis-
tential Dimension.   Philadelphia: Fortress Press, 1967.
229 pp.
   Considers the parables as literature.   General discussion
of literary methodology followed by analyses of selected
parables.   See 8C.16.

8D   Matthew

See also 1C.6; 3J.15; 7B.6; 7C.16.

8D.1   ALBRIGHT, W. F., and C. S. MANN.   Matthew. The Anchor
Bible, 26.   Garden City, New York: Doubleday, 1971.   566 pp.
See 1A.1.

8D.2   BUCHER, GERARD.   "Elements for an Analysis of the Gospel
Text: The Death of Jesus."   Modern Language Notes, 86 (1971),
835-844.
   A structural analysis of Matthew 26-28.   "It is the type of
metamorphosis undergone by the actant-Jesus which confers on

8D   Matthew

him, in the last instance, the heroic vigour and thus raises
him to the realm of values."

8D.3   FARRER, AUSTIN.   St. Matthew and St. Mark.   Second edition.
Westminster: Dacre Press, 1966.   252 pp.
A study of these two Gospels based on the assumption that
"they are literary works and must be interpreted by their
place in a literary history."   Contains some retractions from
his A Study in St. Mark (8E.4).

8D.4   LOHR, CHARLES H.   "Oral Techniques in the Gospel of Matthew."   Catholic Biblical Quarterly, 23 (1961), 403-435.
Studies how Matthew put together his sources by adapting
them to a traditional style, using various oral formulaic devices and arranging his structure.

8D.5   MALINA, BRUCE J.   "The Literary Structure and Form of Matthew 28:16-20."   New Testament Studies, 17 (1970), 87-103.
Studies the literary form and structure of the conclusion
of Matthew's Gospel and the relationship between the Gospel's
beginning and end.

8D.6   STENDAHL, KRISTER.   The School of St. Matthew and Its Use
of the Old Testament.   Philadelphia: Fortress Press, 1968.
263 pp.
Scholarly background on the origin of the Gospel and its
quotations from the Old Testament.   Bibliography.

8D.7   TANNEHILL, ROBERT C.   "The 'Focal Instance' as a Form of
New Testament Speech: A Study of Matthew 5:39b-42."   Journal
of Religion, 50 (1970), 372-385.
Identifies and discusses a type of language in the synoptic
Gospels which is "the focus or point of clarity within a larger field of reference of which the instance is a part" and
cites the four commands in this passage as illustration.

8D.8   WOJCIK, JAN.   "The Two Kingdoms in Matthew's Gospel," in
3F.22, pp. 283-295.
The persona who narrates the Gospel has created a subtle
pattern of emphasis suggesting the two kingdoms; this pattern
shapes the Gospel's narrative.

8E   Mark

See also 3F.17; 3L.5; 7C.16; 7E.8; 7J.3; 8A.7; 8D.3.

The New Testament: Individual Books

8E.1   AUERBACH, ERICH. "Fortunata," in his Mimesis: The Represen-
        tation of Reality in Western Literature. Translated by Wil-
        lard R. Trask. Princeton: Princeton University Press, 1953,
        pp. 24-49.
            Contains discussion of Mark's account of the denial of
        Peter. The New Testament dramatizes a surging up of subsur-
        face layers of experience; thus it must show the responses to
        Christianity of random ordinary people (Peter, the maid, etc.).
        See 3F.45.

8E.2   DANKER, FREDERICK W. "The Literary Unity of Mark 14:1-25."
        Journal of Biblical Literature, 85 (1966), 467-472.
            An advanced study arguing that the key to the unity of this
        passage is found in its allusion to Psalm 40.

8E.3   DEWEY, JOANNA. "The Literary Structure of the Controversy
        Stories in Mark 2:1-3:6." Journal of Biblical Literature, 92
        (1973), 394-401.
            An advanced study arguing that these verses constitute an
        intentional literary subunit within the Gospel.

8E.4   FARRER, AUSTIN. A Study in St. Mark. London: Dacre Press,
        1951. 406 pp.
            Argues for the thematic unity of the Gospel viewing it
        largely as literature. Sees a circular pattern in which Mark
        passes "through a limited round of themes and images, over
        and over again." See 8D.3 for some later retractions.

8E.5   GROS LOUIS, KENNETH R. R. "The Gospel of Mark," in 3F.22,
        pp. 296-329.
            A close reading of the first four chapters followed by a
        consideration of the major themes of the Gospel, the func-
        tions of the parables in the text, and the possible meaning
        of the story as literature.

8E.6   HASHIMOTO, SHIGEO. "The Function of the Old Testament Quo-
        tations and Allusions in the Marcan Passion Narrative." Th.D.
        dissertation, Princeton Theological Seminary, 1970. Abstrac-
        ted in Dissertation Abstracts International, 31 (1971), 4255A.
            The theological implications of these literary allusions.

8E.7   KNIGGE, HEINZ-DIETER. "The Meaning of Mark: The Exegesis
        of the Second Gospel." Interpretation, 22 (1968), 53-70.
            Mark had a definite and unique theological purpose in put-
        ting together his work. Comments on his Gospel's unity.

8E Mark

8E.8   MOORE, CAREY A. "Mark 4:12: More like the Irony of Micaiah
        than Isaiah," in A Light unto My Path: Old Testament Studies
        in Honor of Jacob M. Myers. Edited by Howard N. Bream, Ralph
        D. Heim, and Carey A. Moore. Philadelphia: Temple University
        Press, 1974, pp. 335-344.
            Briefly surveys instances of humor, irony, and sarcasm in
        the Bible and argues that this verse is an example of deliber-
        ate irony: despite later interpretations, Jesus said the exact
        opposite of what he meant.

8E.9   PERRIN, NORMAN. "The Interpretation of the Gospel of Mark."
        Interpretation, 30 (1976), 115-124.
            Surveys modern methods of looking at the Gospel and argues
        the need for reading it now as literature.

8E.10   SCHWEIZER, EDUARD. The Good News according to Mark. Trans-
        lated by Donald H. Madvig. Richmond, Virginia: John Knox
        Press, 1970. 396 pp.
            A verse-by-verse commentary based on Today's English Ver-
        sion (Good News for Modern Man).

8E.11   STAROBINSKI, JEAN. "The Struggle with Legion: A Literary
        Analysis of Mark 5:1-20." Translated by Dan O. Via, Jr. New
        Literary History (University of Virginia), 4 (1973), 331-356.
            A new critical analysis dealing with questions about narra-
        tor, addressee, structure, characters, themes, and the ques-
        tion of interpreting "possession."

8F Luke-Acts

See also 3J.15; 7A.21; 7C.16; 7E.6-7, 9; 8A.6; 8C.2, 5, 7, 15.

8F.1   CADBURY, HENRY J. The Making of Luke-Acts. Second edition.
        London: SPCK, 1961. 397 pp.
            Discusses the personality and purpose of Luke, his ma-
        terials, and his methods. Includes useful information on
        literary types and conventions.

8F.2   DIBELIUS, MARTIN. Studies in the Acts of the Apostles.
        Edited by Heinrich Greeven. London: SCM Press, 1956. 238 pp.
            A collection of scholarly essays written over a number of
        years. Includes material on the style, text, and use of lite-
        rary allusions in Acts.

8F.3   FLENDER, HELMUT. St. Luke: Theologian of Redemptive His-
        tory. Translated by Reginald H. and Ilse Fuller. Philadel-
        phia: Fortress Press, 1967. 191 pp.

This theological study of Luke-Acts contains a chapter describing a particular element of Luke's writing style: parallelism.

8F.4   HUBBARD, BENJAMIN J. "Commissioning Stories in Luke-Acts: A Study of Their Antecedents, Form, and Content." Semeia, 8 (1977), 103-126.
A study of Luke's use of a traditional Near Eastern format for commissioning stories. See 3F.15.

8F.5   JERVELL, JACOB. Luke and the People of God: A New Look at Luke-Acts. Foreword by Nils Dahl. Minneapolis: Augsburg Publishing House, 1972. 207 pp.
A study of several ideas and viewpoints raised in these two biblical books. Provides scholarly background for a study of themes.

8F.6   MUNCK, JOHANNES. The Acts of the Apostles. Revised by William F. Albright and C. S. Mann. The Anchor Bible, 31. Garden City, New York: Doubleday, 1967. 468 pp.
See 1A.1.

8F.7   TANNEHILL, ROBERT C. "The Magnificat as Poem." Journal of Biblical Literature, 93 (1974), 263-275.
A new critical reading of Luke 1:46-55, emphasizing repetitive patterns in the poem.

8G   John

See also 7C.16; 8H.4.

8G.1   BARRETT, C. K. The Gospel according to St. John: An Introduction with Commentary and Notes on the Greek Text. London: SPCK, 1956. 543 pp.
General essays followed by a section-by-section explication.

8G.2   BROWN, RAYMOND E. The Gospel according to John. Two volumes. The Anchor Bible, 29-29A. Garden City, New York: Doubleday, 1966-1970. Volume 29, 684 pp.; volume 29A, 689 pp.
See 1A.1. Volume 29 covers chapters 1-12; volume 29A, chapters 13-21.

8G.3   BULTMANN, RUDOLF. The Gospel of John: A Commentary. Translated by G. R. Beasley-Murray, R. W. N. Hoare, and J. K. Riches. Oxford: Basil Blackwell, 1971. 758 pp.
A line-by-line commentary by a renowned theologian providing background for a literary reading of the Gospel. Bibliography.

8G   John

8G.4   DODD, C. H. The Interpretation of the Fourth Gospel. Cam-
          bridge: Cambridge University Press, 1970. 489 pp.
             Discusses the background leading ideas, and argument and
          structure of the Fourth Gospel.

8G.5   ENZ, JACOB J. "The Book of Exodus as a Literary Type for
          the Gospel of John." Journal of Biblical Literature, 76
          (1957), 208-215.
             John structured his Gospel on the pattern of Exodus to em-
          phasize Jesus as the New Moses.

8G.6   LIGHTFOOT, R. H. St. John's Gospel: A Commentary. Edited
          by C. F. Evans. Oxford: Clarendon Press, 1956. 382 pp.
             An introduction is followed by a section-by-section commen-
          tary. Includes the text of the Revised Version.

8G.7   MARTYN, J. LOUIS. History and Theology in the Fourth Gos-
          pel. New York: Harper & Row, 1968. 190 pp.
             A study of the origin and interpretation of John's Gospel.

8G.8   SMITH, ROBERT HOUSTON. "Exodus Typology in the Fourth Gos-
          pel." Journal of Biblical Literature, 81 (1962), 329-342.
             Sees the structure of John's Gospel as based in part on
          typological allusions to the Old Testament pattern in Exodus
          2:23-12:51.

8G.9   WEAD, DAVID W. The Literary Devices in John's Gospel. A
          Dissertation for the Acquirement of the Degree of Doctor of
          Theology Submitted to the Faculty of Theology of the Univer-
          sity of Basel, Switzerland. Basel: Friedrich Reinhardt Kom-
          missionverlag, 1970. 138 pp.
             A study of such literary devices as point of view, double
          meaning, irony, and metaphor as they appear in the Fourth Gos-
          pel. Bibliography.

8H   The Epistles: General Studies and Non-Pauline Letters

See also 7I.1; 8J.1.

8H.1.   BUCHANAN, GEORGE WESLEY. To the Hebrews. The Anchor Bible,
          36. Garden City, New York: Doubleday, 1972. 301 pp.
             See 1A.1.

8H.2   DOTY, WILLIAM G. Letters in Primitive Christianity.
          Guides to Biblical Scholarship, New Testament Series. Phila-
          delphia: Fortress Press, 1973. 95 pp.

A brief study of the literary form of the epistle in New
Testament times. Chapters on epistolary literature in Hellenism, the Pauline letters, forms within the New Testament epistles, and Early Christian letters. Glossary.

8H.3   REICKE, BO. The Epistles of James, Peter, and Jude. The
Anchor Bible, 37. Garden City, New York: Doubleday, 1964.
259 pp.
         See 1A.1.

8H.4   SALOM, A. P. "Some Aspects of the Grammatical Style of 1
John." Journal of Biblical Literature, 74 (1955), 96-102.
         An advanced study of the style of 1 John in comparison with
the Fourth Gospel. Argues for common authorship.

8I   The Epistles: Paul and the Letters Bearing His Name

See also 3F.26, 32, 45; 7B.6; 7C.16; 7E.2, 6; 7J.3; 8H.

8I.1.   BARTH, MARKUS. Ephesians. Two volumes. The Anchor Bible,
34-34A. Garden City, New York: Doubleday, 1974. Volume 34,
455 pp.; volume 34A, 452 pp.
         See 1A.1. Volume 34 contains the introduction, translation,
and commentary on chapters 1-3. Volume 34A contains the translation and commentary on chapters 4-6.

8I.2   BIAYS, PAUL M. Parallelism in Romans. Fort Hays Studies
(New Series), Literature Series, No. 5. Fort Hays Kansas
State College, 1967. 49 pp.
         Six chapters discuss the general nature of Hebrew poetry
and poetic parallelism. Two more show the influence of this
trait on Paul's prose writing in Romans. Presents a detailed
study of Romans 4. Bibliography.

8I.3   BORNKAMM, GÜNTHER. Paul. Translated by D. M. G. Stalker.
New York: Harper & Row, 1971. 287 pp.
         A study of the Apostle's life, work, gospel, and theology.

8I.4   DIBELIUS, MARTIN, and WERNER GEORG KÜMMEL. Paul. Translated by Frank Clarke. Philadelphia: Westminster Press, 1953.
180 pp.
         A study of the Apostle and his work providing background
for his contributions to, and role in, the New Testament.

8I.5   FRANCIS, FRED O., and J. PAUL SAMPLEY, eds. Pauline Parallels. Philadelphia: Fortress Press, 1975. 398 pp.

8I The Epistles

A reference tool printing thematically related passages in the epistles in parallel columns. Uses the Common Bible (Revised Standard Version).

8I.6   HAUGHTON, ROSEMARY. Paul and the World's Most Famous Letters. Nashville: Abingdon Press, 1970. 110 pp.
Provides background and context on each of the Pauline letters for the general reader. Illustrations and bibliography.

8I.7   HUNTER, ARCHIBALD M. Interpreting Paul's Gospel. Philadelphia: Westminster Press, 1954. 144 pp.
Background on Paul's theology and its relevance for the twentieth century.

8I.8   KINNEY, LAURENCE F. "Studia Biblica 31: The Pastoral Epistles." Interpretation, 9 (1955), 429-435.
Background on 1 and 2 Timothy and Titus including a stylistic analysis to show that they are not Paul's writing.

8I.9   KLAUSNER, JOSEPH. From Jesus to Paul. Translated by William F. Stinespring. New York: Macmillan, 1944. 640 pp.
Background on and a study of the life and teachings of Paul, written by a Jew. Part of a trilogy including 7A.16 and 8B.6.

8I.10   KNOX, JOHN. Chapters in a Life of Paul. New York: Abingdon Press, 1950. 168 pp.
An advanced study of some of the problems to be encountered by one who would reconstruct a biography of Paul from the New Testament.

8I.11   KNOX, RONALD. "St. Paul," in 3B.3, pp. 104-109.
A brief character sketch of Paul based on the Epistles.

8I.12   MEEKS, WAYNE A., ed. The Writings of St. Paul. Norton Critical Edition. New York: W. W. Norton, 1972. 471 pp.
The text of the letters attributed to Paul (Revised Standard Version) with introductions and annotations. Also contains an extensive collection of critical articles representing views of Paul and his influence in several areas. Selected bibliography.

8I.13   MUGGERIDGE, MALCOLM, and ALEC VIDLER. Paul, Envoy Extraordinary. London: Collins, 1972. 159 pp.
A dialogue based on a BBC film tracing the life and work of Paul. Illustrations.

8I.14   ORR, WILLIAM F., and JAMES ARTHUR WALTHER. 1 Corinthians. The Anchor Bible, 32. Garden City, New York: Doubleday, 1976. 408 pp.

See 1A.1.   The introduction includes a life of Paul.

8I.15   REUMANN, JOHN.   "St. Paul's Use of Irony."   Lutheran Quarterly, 7 (1955), 140-145.
          Cites examples of Pauline phrases in which "the meaning
intended is contrary to that seemingly expressed."

8I.16   ROBINSON, JAMES M.   "A Formal Analysis of Colossians 1:15-
20."   Journal of Biblical Literature, 76 (1957), 270-287.
          A form-critical analysis providing clues to the literary
structure of the passage.

8I.17   ROETZEL, CALVIN J.   The Letters of Paul: Conversations in
Context.   Atlanta: John Knox Press, 1975.   124 pp.
          An introduction for the nonspecialist providing background
on the nature and contexts of the Epistles.   Includes a chapter on Paul's use of myth (chapter 5, pp. 69-80).

8I.18   SANDERS, ED PARISH.   "Literary Dependence in Colossians."
Journal of Biblical Literature, 85 (1966), 28-45.
          An advanced study of parallels between Colossians and the
undisputed Pauline letters.   Attempts to establish authorship.

8I.19   VIA, DAN O., JR.   "A Structuralist Approach to Paul's Old
Testament Hermeneutic."   Interpretation, 28 (1974), 201-220.
          Studies Paul's use of a context created by his hearers'
familiarity with Deuteronomy and by "the/a comic genre, which
is a structure of the human mind."   See 3L.4.

8J   Revelation

See also 3E.20; 3I.2; 4H; 7E.6.

8J.1   BOWMAN, JOHN WICK.   The First Christian Drama: The Book of
Revelation.   Philadelphia: Westminster Press, 1968.   159 pp.
          Originally entitled The Drama of the Book of Revelation
(1955).   This reading sees the book as a play with the literary form of a letter superimposed on it.   Each "scene" is
paraphrased and commented on.   The result is seen as "a clear
statement of the Gospel--how God through the ages works for
man's salvation."

8J.2   CAIRD, G. B.   A Commentary on the Revelation of St. John
the Divine.   New York: Harper & Row, 1966.   326 pp.
          An original translation and passage-by-passage commentary
with ancillary material.   Bibliography.

8J   Revelation

8J.3   CARTER, FREDERICK. "Drama and Apocalypse." Life and Letters, 60 (1949), 221-229.
         Sees Revelation as a drama "arranged for performance by a
protagonist with a chorus, besides masks and mimes."

8J.4   FARRER, AUSTIN. A Rebirth of Images: The Making of St.
John's Apocalpyse. Gloucester, Massachusetts: Peter Smith,
1970. 350 pp.
         A reading of Revelation based on the assumption that it is
"a great and vividly imagined poem, in which the whole world
of that age's faith is bodied forth." Includes a complete
text of the book.

8J.5   FIORENZA, ELISABETH. "The Eschatology and Composition of
the Apocalpyse." Catholic Biblical Quarterly, 30 (1968),
537-569.
         A study of "the composition and the purpose of the Apoca-
lypse . . . in an attempt to show how the ecclesiology and the
eschatology determine the structure of the book."

8J.6   FORD, J. MASSYNGBERDE. Revelation. The Anchor Bible, 38.
Garden City, New York: Doubleday, 1975. 504 pp.
         See 1A.1.

8J.7   GROS LOUIS, KENNETH R. R. "Revelation," in 3F.22, pp. 330-
345.
         A reading suggesting that the book is a consciously unified
work, commenting on (among other things) the limits of human
imagination: "some things in the universe . . . will remain
inexpressible. . . ."

8J.8   KALLAS, JAMES. "The Apocalypse--An Apocalyptic Book?"
Journal of Biblical Literature, 86 (1967), 69-80.
         Revelation is unlike other apocalyptic books because of its
attitude toward suffering. See reply by Bruce W. Jones, "More
about the Apocalypse as Apocalyptic," in the same journal, 87
(1968), 325-327.

8J.9   KEPLER, THOMAS S. The Book of Revelation: A Commentary for
Laymen. New York: Oxford University Press, 1957. 242 pp.
         An introduction and passage-by-passage commentary, reprint-
ing the Revised Standard Version. Designed for the nonspecialist. Bibliography.

8J.10   KERMODE, FRANK. The Sense of an Ending: Studies in the
Theory of Fiction. New York: Oxford University Press, 1967.
199 pp., passim.

A series of lectures studying the structure of fiction in relation to the ways we have imagined the ends of the world. Background on apocalyptic literature with some commentary on Revelation itself.

8J.11   LAWRENCE, D. H. Apocalypse. With an introduction by Richard Aldington. The Phoenix Edition of D. H. Lawrence. London: William Heinemann, 1972. 128 pp.
First published in 1931. The famous novelist's unorthodox reading of Revelation as "the expression of frustrated power-lust." See the personal memoir on Lawrence and his interpretation by Helen Corke in Lawrence and "Apocalypse" (London: William Heinemann, 1933).

8J.12   MINEAR, PAUL S. I Saw a New Earth: An Introduction to the Visions of the Apocalypse. Washington, D.C.: Corpus Books, 1968. 411 pp.
This commentary, while acknowledging John as a literary artist, focuses on the universal meaning of Revelation for Christians. Includes a detailed analysis of six visions, scholarly essays on themes and images, and a new translation. Bibliography.

Index

Titles of the books of the Bible are capitalized. For other guides to the use of the Index, see the Introduction.

Dodd, C. H., 3D.4; 7B.5-6; 8C.8; 8G.4

Dolan, John P., 7A.7

Dornisch, Loretta, 3L.1

Doty, William G., 3L.2-3; 8C.5; 8H.2

Douay-Rheims (Challoner) Version, editions of, 1A.16, 21; reviews and stylistic analyses of, 1C.4, 24

Douglas, J. D., 2E.6

Downing Christine, 5D.6

Drama, 3F.44; 3M.11; 4I.1; 5L.2, 31; 8J.1, 3. See also Comedy; Tragedy

Drijvers, Pius, 5M.8

Driver, Godfrey R., 1D.13; 4D.4

Driver, Samuel Rolles, 4E.8; 5L.5

Dwight, Timothy. See 3E.5

ECCLESIASTES, 50

ECCLESTIASTICUS, 4B.11. See also 6C; 6E

Eichrodt, Walther, 4B.2

Eissfeldt, Otto, 4C.8

Eliade, Mircea, 3J.4-5

Eliot, T. S., 1C.9; 3D.5

Elliott, Melvin E., 2F.3

Ellison, John W., 2G.2

Encyclopedias, biblical, 2E

Engel, Walburga von Raffler, 8C.14

English, G. Schuyler, 1A.20

Enz, Jacob J., 8G.5

EPHESIANS, EPISTLE TO THE. See 8I, esp. 8I.1

Epic, 4F.7; 4I.3; 5I.8; 5L.37

Epistles, the, bearing Paul's name, 8I; general studies of, 8H; non-Pauline letters, 8H

Eppstein, Victor, 1C.10

ESDRAS, 6F.5. See also 6C; 6E

ESTHER, 5K

ESTHER (THE APOCRYPHAL ADDITIONS), 6F.4. See also 6C; 6E

Etheridge, Eugene W., 3F.12

Evans, Bergen, 1C.11-12

Evans, C. F., 1D.7; 8G.6

Evans, Cornelia, 1C.12

Evil, literary theme of, 3F.1; 4I.10; 5B.7; 5L.15, 41; 5M.2

EXODUS, 5D

EZEKIEL, 5U

EZRA, 5J

Fairy tales, 3G.9; 4I.5; 7H.3

Farmer, William Reuben, 7A.8; 8A.5

Farrer, Austin, 8D.3; 8E.4; 8J.4

Fawcett, Thomas, 7H.1

Feldman, Herman, 1B.9

Fenton, John, 7C.16

Ferguson, George, 3F.13

Filson, Floyd Vivian, 2D.8; 7G.1

Fine, Hillel A., 5L.6

Finegan, Jack, 2C.4

Fiorenza, Elisabeth, 8J.5

Fisher, Robert W., 3A.4

Fitzmyer, Joseph A., 2H.4

Fixler, Michael, 1B.21

Flender, Helmut, 8F.3

Fletcher, Angus, 3I.1

Fokkelman, J. P., 5A.1

Folklore, 3F.44; 4D.6; 4F.1; 4I.4, 6; 5D.9; 5L.43; 7D.2. See also Myth

Forbes, Cheryl, 3F.14

Ford, J. Massyngberde, 8J.6

Fox, Everett, 5X.2

Francis, Fred O., 8I.5

Frank, Harry Thomas, 2C.5

Frank, Joseph, 1B.11

Frankfort, H. A., 4D.5

Frankfort, Henri, 4A.4; 4D.5

Frazer, James G., 3J.6; 4I.4, 6

Freedman, David Noel, 1A.1; 2C.9; 3H.3; 5D.7; 5L.7; 5M.9

Freeman, James M., 2I.3

Frei, Hans W., 3E.4

Freimarck, Vincent, 1C.13; 3E.5

Fretheim, Terence E., 5M.10

Freud, Sigmund, 5D.8

Friess, Horace L., 1B.4

Fritsch, Charles T., 5C.5

Froehlich, Karlfried, 3E.6; 7C.10

Fromm, Erich, 4B.3; 4I.5

Frost, Stanley Brice, 1D.14; 4H.1

Frye, Northrop, 3J.7-10; 5L.8

Frye, Roland Mushat, 1B.12

Fuller, Reginald C., 2H.7

Fuller, Reginald H., 2H.15; 7C.4

Index

Sherwin-White, A. N., 7A.21
Shoham, S. Giora, 5C.9
Sidney, Philip, 3E.21
Simile, 4D.19, 23; 5W.3
Simon, Ulrich, 3G.7
Simon, Uriel, 5I.10
Skehan, Patrick W., 4B.11
Skilton, John Hamilton, 1C.32
Smalley, Beryl, 3E.22
Smend, Rudolf, 4A.21
Smith, D. Moody, Jr., 7E.14
Smith, George Adam, 4A.22
Smith, J. M. Powis, 1A.2
Smith, Morton, 8A.6
Smith, Robert Houston, 8G.8
Snaith, Norman H., 5L.41
Soggin, J. Alberto, 4C.29
SONG OF SONGS, 5P
Speiser, E. A., 5A.7
Spiegelberg, Friedrich, 1B.4
Spitzer, Gary, 3M.10
Spivack, Charlotte, 5L.42
Spivey, Robert A., 3L.4; 7E.14
Sprau, George, 3F.37
Starobinski, Jean, 3L.5; 8E.11
Stegner, W. Richard, 7B.7; 8A.11
Stendahl, Krister, 6D.8; 8D.6
Sternberg, Meir, 3G.8; 5I.6-7
Stevenson, William Barron,
   5L.43-44
Stibbs, A. M., 2H.9
Strachan, James, 1D.39
Strong, James, 2G.3
Structuralist approaches, to the
   Bible, 3L; to the New Testa-
   ment, 7J; to the Old Testa-
   ment, 4K
Style (in the Bible itself),
   4E.15; 4F.7; 4G.8; 5A.1;
   5B.2-3; 5C.1; 5D.12; 5G.1;
   5M.6, 9, 11; 50.2-3; 5S.5,
   7; 7E.4; 8D.4; 8F.2; 8H.3;
   8I.8
Style (in the English Bible), 1C
Suffering, literary theme of,
   3C.4; 4B.6; 5L.13, 15, 26-27,
   44; 8J.8
Suggs, M. Jack, 1A.18
Super, A. S., 5W.3
Sutcliffe, Edmund F., 3C.4
Swaim, J. Carter, 1B.1

Sweet, John, 1B.2
Sykes, Norman, 1D.40
Symbolism, 3F.1, 3, 6, 9, 13, 27,
   39; 3H.2; 3I.1; 3J.14; 3K.6;
   4I.5; 5B.1; 7I.4. See also
   Typology
Synoptic Gospels, 8A.1-3, 5, 8,
   10, 13; 8D.7
Sypherd, Wilber Owen, 3F.38

Talmon, S., 3F.1
Tannehill, Robert C., 7I.2; 8D.7;
   8F.7
Tarn, W. W., 6A.3
Tasker, R. V. G., 1D.41
Taylor, Vincent, 8A.12
Tempest, Norton R., 1C.33
Terrien, Samuel, 5L.45; 5M.23
Themes, literary. See 2I.5;
   3F.23; 3H.4; 4D.9; 4I.13;
   5D.1; 5G.4; 5L.33; 5M.12, 20,
   25; 5U.2; 6F.1; 8E.4-5, 11;
   8F.5; 8J.12. See also Death;
   Evil; God; Love; Man; Motifs;
   Suffering
Theological background. See
   Scholarly and theological
   background
THESSALONIANS, EPISTLES TO THE.
   See 8I
Thomas, D. Winton, 4D.12; 4J.2
THOMAS, THE GOSPEL OF, 3F.26
Thompson, Craig R., 1D.42
Thompson, Dorothy, 1C.34
Thompson, Francis, 3E.23
Thompson, Leonard L., 3K.5
Throckmorton, Burton H., Jr.,
   8A.13
TIMOTHY, EPISTLES TO. See 8I,
   esp. 8I.8
TITUS, EPISTLE TO. See 8I, esp.
   8I.8
Tkacik, Arnold J., 1A.18
TOBIT, 4E.26; 4F.2. See also
   6C; 6E
Today's English Version, 1A.4
Tolbert, Mary Ann, 8C.7
Tolkien, J. R. R., 7H.3
Torah, 3D.11; 3E.19; 4A.10; 7A.5.
   See also Law; Pentateuch